A WARRIOR'S GUIDE
TO PSYCHOLOGY
AND PERFORMANCE

A WARRIOR'S GUIDE TO PSYCHOLOGY AND PERFORMANCE

What You Should Know About Yourself and Others

GEORGE MASTROIANNI, BARBARA PALMER,
DAVID PENETAR, AND VICTORIA TEPE

Potomac Books, Inc.
Washington, D.C.

Library of Congress Cataloging-in-Publication Data
A warrior's guide to psychology and performance : what you should know about yourself and others / George Mastroianni ... [et al.]. — 1st ed.
   p. cm.
  Includes bibliographical references and index.
  ISBN 978-1-59797-545-2 (pbk. : alk. paper)
  1. Psychology, Military. 2. Combat—Psychological aspects. 3. Performance—Psychological aspects. 4. Stress (Psychology) 5. Soldiers—Mental health—United States. I. Mastroianni, George.
  U22.3.W368 2010
  355.001'9—dc22

                                            2010035150

Potomac Books, Inc.
22841 Quicksilver Drive
Dulles, Virginia 20166

First Edition

10 9 8 7 6 5 4 3 2

CONTENTS

FOREWORD

The story goes that an ancient ruler called for engineers to build a bridge to join together the halves of her kingdom that were separated by a deep chasm. The first engineer to seek an audience presented himself before her and requested to be named her chief for the endeavor. The ruler asked the engineer, "With what would you build my bridge?" The engineer replied, "Strong timbers of bamboo, your majesty." The ruler thought for a moment and dismissed the engineer without comment. The second engineer presented himself to the ruler and was asked the same question. "Pillars of granite, your majesty." He, too, was dismissed, along with scores of engineers, all of whom proposed building the bridge with various combinations of the strongest materials available in the land. Finally, a soldier from the ruler's palace guard presented himself to her majesty and, like the others, was asked, "With what would you build my bridge?" The soldier looked at his ruler and said, "Your majesty, your bridge will be built with people, well led." The ruler appointed the soldier the chief of engineers, and so the bridge was built.

We build our bridges, fight our wars, sail our ships, fly our drones, and accomplish our missions with people. Service in the warrior clan is an inherently human endeavor. Soldiers, sailors, airmen, and Marines are the very essence of our national defense. This fact places the discipline most central to the human dimension—psychology—at the core of the warrior's art and science. Whether you are in basic training on your first enlistment or a flag officer commanding legions of service members, understanding yourself and the people with whom you live and fight is key. Without this understanding, service members cannot and will not perform at their best. An underperforming military is an unpleasant and dangerous place to live and work. More importantly, an underperforming military is a threat to our country because our military takes action to sustain our democracy every single day.

This book, and the knowledge about psychology it shares, will help you live a better life in the service. Knowing what is between the covers of this book will help you perform better, experience less stress, recover from trauma, develop resilience, enjoy your time in the service more, and be better in your relationships with other people. Psychology informs every dimension of your life. When you equip yourself with knowledge about psychology, it's a kit you take with you wherever you go—and that's a real value to service members, who will be asked to go almost anywhere and do almost anything.

Traditionally, though, most service schools equip their service members with far too limited a psychological kit, concentrating largely on training skills and abilities. Owing to the economies of time and money, most people in the military go about their professional lives less prepared for their service experience than they might otherwise be. As a consequence, the leadership of our armed forces is consumed with reactions to persistent problems in the human dimension. Issues of combat effectiveness, career retention, lack of motivation, domestic violence, alcohol and substance abuse, bigotry toward others, post-traumatic stress, suicide, risky behaviors, atrocities, and hate crimes come with an enormous cost in terms of effectiveness, money, and human suffering. There are training programs directed in reaction to all these problems, but they are focused on specific issues, and that means that knowledge about psychology is offered only on a "by exception" basis in training focused on problems, not people. The book you are reading is important and unique because it comes at these issues from an opposite approach. It will better equip you for a positive experience as you serve, and it will help you to avoid the common problems as a by-product. As such, this little book makes a powerful statement that people are as important as the problems they sometimes cause. It fills an education gap in a training culture.

In filling the education gap, this book ascends to moral high ground. The leadership of our armed forces—indeed the American public—has a moral obligation to prepare warriors for whatever we ask them to face. In World War II, every American sacrificed resources to enable the country to equip the fighting forces. In contemporary times, when we have recognized deficiencies in vehicle survivability, body armor, or other equipment vital to the lives of warriors, there has been public outcry because of the moral imperative of equipping fighting forces with the best our society has to offer. Equipping our forces with science-based knowledge about themselves and others is no less a moral imperative. It is simply the right thing to do.

One of the real delights in reading this book is in imagining where this book will go. In a practical sense, it was designed with a view toward economy and portability so that it will find its way into rucksacks, duffle bags, and cargo pockets—convenient to the people who read it. I find myself envisioning it tucked into a helmet bag on the back of a helicopter seat, sitting in post clinic waiting rooms, being read by Humvee drivers while they wait during meetings, and being used by sergeants in professional development sessions. Being a soldier myself for more than thirty years, thinking about this book and envisioning its impact around the globe is extremely satisfying.

If you are a soldier, sailor, airman, or Marine, you've volunteered to serve our country side by side with your fellow Americans. Thank you for choosing to serve. This book may act as a battle buddy to you as you think through things as simple as how to hang with the heat to things as complex as why you might have chosen the profession of arms as your calling. The field of psychology is unique in its ability to inform and educate service members and their families about the lifestyle we lead in the warrior clan. Make it work for you. Use it to reflect on—and adapt to—this priceless chapter in the story of your life.

Col. Tom Kolditz, PhD
Department of Behavioral Sciences and Leadership
West Point, New York
Author of *In Extremis Leadership: Leading As If Your Life Depended On It*

ACKNOWLEDGMENTS

In 1948 Marjorie Van de Water[1] described the challenges of writing about scientific discoveries in a way that is accessible and useful to non-scientists. As evidence that this could be done, she referred specifically to the books she had coedited and published during World War II:

> During the war, we conducted a new experiment in public education. In a few books, published in pocket-size, paper-bound, editions that would cost only twenty-five cents a copy, we put the content of college textbooks in science. They were written without any technical terminology, in a way designed to be interesting as well as informative. Intended especially for men in the armed services, they were beamed at intelligent adults who have no special training in the sciences.[2]

Van de Water described these efforts as a "community writing" process that made it possible for one small book to include expert knowledge drawn from scientific authorities across a wide range of subject matter areas.

> Many people said it couldn't be done. They warned us that contributors would be angry at having their work re-written so that they could hardly recognize it. On the contrary, most of them were enthusiastic and proud at having taken part in such a joint effort. It was undoubtedly more successful than a book of the same sort would have been written by any one of those who contributed to the project.

The book you hold in your hand now was inspired by those earlier efforts by Marjorie Van de Water, E. V. McCollum, and other well-known behavioral scientists who collaborated to write and publish *Psychology for the Fighting Man* (1943), *Psychology for the Returning Serviceman* (1945), and other such books during World War II. In keeping with their original purpose and process, we adopted a similar approach. We gathered guidance, insight, and expert knowledge from numerous military and civilian scientific advisers and subject matter experts in the behavioral and medical sciences. Their knowledge and perspectives were collected, organized, rewritten, reorganized, edited and reedited, and sometimes rewritten and reedited yet again to achieve a concise and, we hope, useful presentation of biobehavioral science related to military performance. Consistent with Van de Water's advice, we've kept it short. We've tried to avoid "useless words." We do not try to be popular. We draw on all that we know, think, and feel as a community of colleagues.

This book represents the dedicated commitment and combined expertise of military and civilian scientists who share a common commitment to improve the health, well-being, and effectiveness of all men and women who serve in the U.S. military. We wish to extend our deepest appreciation to all who served as core working group members, project planners, subject matter experts and advisers, thought composers, content organizers, and information hunter-gatherers in support of this uniquely collaborative effort.

Special thanks go to Col. Brian Lukey and Lt. Col. Carl Hover for their leadership and support throughout, and to Col. Thomas Kolditz and Col. Karl Friedl for creative guidance, wisdom, and consistent encouragement to overcome.

In alphabetical order and by service branch, we therefore acknowledge and thank:

UNITED STATES AIR FORCE

Col. Rick L. Campise, Langley Air Force Base
George Mastroianni, U.S. Air Force Academy

UNITED STATES ARMY

Amy B. Adler, Walter Reed Army Institute of Research
Nehama Babin, U.S. Army Research Institute for Behavioral and Social Sciences

James Belanich, U.S. Army Research Institute for Behavioral and Social Sciences

Maj. Jeffrey Bergmann, U.S. Military Academy at West Point

Col. Carl A. Castro, Walter Reed Army Institute of Research

Yung (May) Chen, U.S. Military Academy at West Point

Col. Karl E. Friedl, Telemedicine and Advanced Technology Research Center

Paul A. Gade, U.S. Army Research Institute for Behavioral and Social Sciences

Gerald Goodwin, U.S. Army Research Institute for Behavioral and Social Sciences

Peter Greenston, U.S. Army Research Institute for Behavioral and Social Sciences

Col. James Griffith, Medical Service Corps, U.S. Army National Guard

Lt. Col. David Grossman (ret.), Killology Research Group

Lt. Col. Carl Hover (ret.), U.S. Army Medical Research and Materiel Command

Katherine M. Jenkins, Maryland Air and Army National Guard

Col. Thomas Kolditz, U.S. Military Academy at West Point

Jessica Lang, Walter Reed Army Institute of Research

Col. Brian Lukey, U.S. Army Medical Research and Materiel Command

Capt. Bret A. Moore, 85th Combat Stress Control Detachment

Lt. Col. James W. Ness, U.S. Military Academy at West Point

Col. David Penetar (ret.), McLean Hospital/Harvard Medical School

Zita M. Simutis (ret.), U.S. Army Research Institute for Behavioral and Social Sciences

Maj. Melba Stetz, Tripler Army Medical Center

Col. Patrick Sweeney, U.S. Military Academy at West Point

Kathleen M. Wright, Walter Reed Army Institute of Research

UNITED STATES NAVY AND MARINE CORPS

Mary E. Campise, U.S. Marine Corps Headquarters

Lt. Michael J. Franks, Naval Hospital Pensacola

Cdr. Gary B. Hoyt, 1st Marine Division, Camp Pendleton

W. Brad Johnson, U.S. Naval Academy

Cdr. David E. Jones, Naval Medical Center Portsmouth

Lt. Cdr. Carrie H. Kennedy, Naval Aerospace Medical Institute
Anna Simons, Naval Postgraduate School

OTHERS

Jane Arabian, Office of the Undersecretary of Defense for Personnel and
   Readiness
Bradford Booth, Caliber, an ICF International Company
Nathaniel Frank, University of California, Santa Barbara
Barbara Palmer, Survivability and Vulnerability Information Analysis
   Center
Mady W. Segal, University of Maryland, College Park
Victoria Tepe, Survivability and Vulnerability Information Analysis Center
Frank M. Webbe, Florida Institute of Technology

VOLUME EDITORS

George Mastroianni, U.S. Air Force Academy
Barbara Palmer, Survivability/Vulnerability Information Analysis Center
David Penetar, McLean Hospital/Harvard Medical School
Victoria Tepe, Survivability/Vulnerability Information Analysis Center

The material contained herein is the responsibility of the editors and does
not necessarily represent the official position of any U.S. government entity or
agency.

INTRODUCTION

This is not the first book of its kind. During World War II, prominent behavioral and military scientists also collaborated to produce similar practical books designed specifically "for the fighting man himself." Those books—entitled *Psychology for the Fighting Man* (1943) and *Psychology for the Returning Serviceman* (1945)—were based upon the most advanced science of the time. They were motivated by commitment to the national defense and were published as a contribution to the war effort. Each book gave military members and families direct access to the best available expert information in understandable and practical form. During and after World War II, several hundred thousand copies were printed and distributed to U.S. soldiers, sailors, airmen, and Marines.

Modern behavioral science offers a wealth of knowledge that can be put to practical use in meeting the daily demands of professional military life and service today. The purpose of *A Warrior's Guide to Psychology and Performance* is to make relevant information easily accessible—as it was during World War II—in the form of a timely, well-organized, and practical guide for today's military professional. This book represents the collaborative contributions of dedicated military and civilian subject matter experts. Each chapter addresses specific demands of military life and service. In each case, expert contributors have emphasized specific skills, strategies, behavior, and support measures that the reader can apply to benefit his or her own overall psychological health, resilience, job performance, longevity, and survival. Throughout this book, an effort has also been made to address the additional, sometimes unique concerns of reserve duty

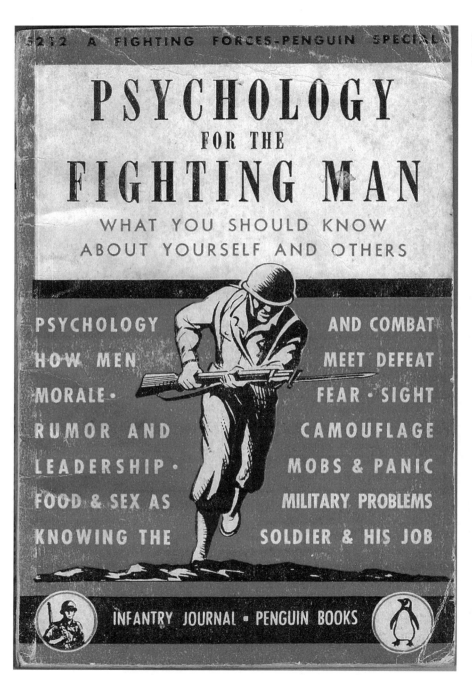

PSYCHOLOGY
FOR THE
FIGHTING MAN

WHAT YOU SHOULD KNOW
ABOUT YOURSELF AND OTHERS

PSYCHOLOGY	AND COMBAT
HOW MEN	MEET DEFEAT
MORALE ·	FEAR · SIGHT
RUMOR AND	CAMOUFLAGE
LEADERSHIP ·	MOBS & PANIC
FOOD & SEX AS	MILITARY PROBLEMS
KNOWING THE	SOLDIER & HIS JOB

INFANTRY JOURNAL · PENGUIN BOOKS

During World War II, military and civilian researchers collaborated to create practical books based on the best science of the time. Copies were distributed to educate and support American service members and their families.

military members. You do not have to read the chapters of this book in order. Each chapter makes sense by itself, and each chapter may be of more or less interest to you at different times throughout your military service.

Chapter 1, "Adjustment to Military Life and Service," is intended to guide the expectations of new military personnel. Here you will find essential information in subject areas such as military standards, organizational perspective, diversity, teamwork, leadership, training, and military family life. Chapter 2, "Your Body and Your Mind," and Chapter 3, "Understanding and Dealing with Stress," contain psychological and other scientific knowledge that is vital to your success at all stages of military life and service. To be the best warfighter you can be, you should understand how processes in your body can affect how you think, what you feel, and how well you do your job. Chapter 2 considers essential relationships between mind and body, emphasizing the role of sensory systems, nutrition, physical fitness, sleep, stress, and performance in harsh environments.

Chapter 3 focuses specifically on how to deal with stress, beginning with an essential review of current scientific knowledge about how the human body and brain respond to stress. This chapter is essential reading for the warfighter who wants to understand how stress affects performance and how to become more resilient to stress.

Chapter 4, "Surviving and Thriving in Combat," speaks to specific concerns of warfighters after deployment and in combat through the lens of American military history and contemporary demands of war. Chapter 5, "From Combat to Home," addresses the often challenging process of returning home and readjusting to "normal" life after combat. Because this chapter sheds light on potential difficulties often met in the transition from combat to home, its content may also be valuable to family members, friends, and colleagues.

At the end of the book, we have included an Appendix of Resources to assist the reader in locating additional helpful readings, books, programs, and services.

American soldiers are known the world over for their resilience and adaptability. In writing this book, we were challenged to provide useful information about how to face and deal with possible negative effects of combat-related stress while also emphasizing that most warfighters will not experience significant difficulties as the result of their combat experiences. It is important for the reader to understand that serious combat-related stress reactions are neither expected nor desirable, and that when they occur, they are not the result of individual weakness or fault.

Not all warfighters will be psychologically challenged by combat. Many will return home in good physical and psychological health. However, to prepare for the future and prevent potential problems, it is important that the reader be given access to useful information about what to expect. Sometimes problems cannot be avoided: the information we have included in this book is intended to help the reader recognize such situations if they do occur and recover effectively from them.

Therefore, we have chosen to acknowledge and discuss the possible psychological effects of stress as openly as we consider how stress might affect overall physical health and performance. We offer basic guidance to support prevention by self-help, early recognition of warning signs and symptoms, and encouragement to seek help when necessary. Our intent is to encourage a proactive approach to improving performance and survivability.

The more you know about your natural capacities and limitations, the better prepared you will be to adapt to change and respond to challenge. Your success as an individual and as a military professional can be enhanced and ensured by correct knowledge about how you function physically, mentally, and socially. In difficult situations, good decisions must be guided by your knowledge of self and others, and by the lessons of military history. This book is intended to provide such critical knowledge, drawn from research and experience and selected for its practical usefulness to American warfighters.

The Authors and Editors

CHAPTER ONE

Adjustment to Military Life and Service

If you are new to the military, it may seem difficult at first to find your sense of place within a very large organization. Here, we offer guidance toward adjustment to life in the military. First, we will consider how life in the military can be different from life as a civilian. Then we will present basic demographic information that may help you to see yourself as an important part of a larger organization of uniquely qualified people. We will discuss things you can do to serve as a team member and how you can improve your skills through training and continued learning opportunities. We will consider issues that relate to gender, race, and sexual orientation. Finally, we will address the importance of family support and talk about how the military supports its members' families.

ADJUSTING TO THE MILITARY PERSPECTIVE

Every new member of today's military is a volunteer. However, once you join the armed services, you must obey many rules. As soon as you begin your training as a new recruit, you are trained to think not only in terms of what is best for you as an individual but also in terms of what is best for your unit and its mission. More than any other aspect or appearance of military life and culture, this is what will distinguish you from most civilians. Of course, there are also many other unique demands of military service. The military will take care of your needs—food, shelter, education, and income—but will also hold you accountable for everything you do, both on duty and off.

The military is organized as a strict hierarchy. Every service member holds a rank, and with each different rank comes a specific set of duties, responsi-

Combat Logistics Regiment 27 company formation, Camp Al Taqaddum, Iraq. *U.S. Marine Corps photograph by Lance Cpl. Melissa A. Latty*

bilities, obligations, expectations, privileges, and opportunities. The military is an enormous bureaucracy that at times may seem very impersonal. However, military life promotes cohesion and the development of close, lifelong friendships. Service members spend a great deal of time together, often in close quarters and sometimes under difficult conditions. Combat is an especially stressful experience. Those who serve in combat together often remain close friends for the rest of their lives.

Members of the U.S. armed services are judged primarily and fairly on the merits of their performance, including attitude, effort, aptitude, stamina, and the ability to work well with others. If you are new to the job, you will not be expected to perform new skills until you've been trained. Most tests will require you to meet an objective standard of performance. The idea is that you should compete against yourself, not against your peers.

As a new recruit, most of what you are taught will probably be very new to you. Very few people join the military already knowing how to shoot a crew-served weapon or prepare a meal for hundreds of other people. How much effort you invest will matter a great deal at this point. Military trainers and leaders recognize that individuals learn at different rates and no one can learn or excel

Airmen at Vandenberg Air Force Base simulate an enemy attack during a pre-deployment training exercise. *U.S. Air Force photo/Airman 1st Class Kerelin Molina*

at everything equally. Above all, you will be observed and judged in terms of how hard you try and how hard you work. The assumption is that if you give it your best effort, your skills will improve over time.

On entering the military, you will quickly observe one of the most obvious differences between the military and much of civilian life. In the military, there is constant awareness of interdependency. You will almost always be in the company of your peers or immediate supervisors. You will know, as your peers know, that the success and survival of every unit depends on the dedicated performance of each and every one of its members.

Although military life and service is very much about following rules, honoring structure, and obeying orders, it is also an experience that many people find to be very liberating. Military training and service will expose you to physical challenges and skill sets that aren't available as civilian experiences. As a result, service members gain a unique sense of confidence, capacity, and self-sufficiency. Many also discover talents and capacities they may never have otherwise known. As a member of the military, you will meet people and see places and be exposed to standards and role models that will almost certainly change your life in positive ways you could never have anticipated as a civilian.

U.S. Air Force Academy cadets practice the low crawl as part of basic training. *U.S. Air Force photo/ Master Sgt. Scott Reed*

Military service can also be dangerous, even during peacetime. It is essential that you are vigilant and work to sustain your proficiency at all times, remembering that even in a comparatively safe noncombat environment, accidents sometimes happen. It can be a challenge to maintain peak performance during prolonged periods of boredom. You will probably experience such periods of boredom from time to time. Remember that you have a job to do and a duty to do it well no matter what else might be happening (or not happening).

As a member of the military, there may be times when you receive orders without explanation. You may not understand the purpose of what you are doing. You must simply accept that there is a good reason for what you've been ordered to do. Different people deal with this in different ways. For some, complaining relieves frustration. Others prefer to engage in passionate debate about how things might be done differently. Because military life is an all-consuming investment of time, energy, and effort, service members can become very passionate in their opinions about how things are done and how they think things should be done. This is understandable and usually healthy, but it is also important to maintain a sense of humor.

If you can keep and express a sense of humor about yourself and your surroundings, others will find it easier to hear and understand what you have to say. Humor helps relieve boredom, frustration, and fear. Humor provides a healthy basis for friendship. Not everyone can be a comedian, but if you can laugh through difficult times, you will find it easier to adjust and cope with new situations and demands.

When you joined the military, you did not give up your personality. You are still an individual with unique strengths, weaknesses, characteristics, experiences, needs, and talents. The U.S. military needs you to bring your unique strengths, talents, and interests to the task of being a warfighter. Life in the military will provide you with opportunities to build upon your strengths, compensate for your weaknesses, accept new responsibilities, and mature as an individual.

Finally, it is important to note that your individual experience as a service member may depend to some degree on your branch of service, unit, or job assignment. Each service branch has its own sense of identity, history, and culture. There is healthy tension between the different branches, but they coexist in joint service to the nation. Within each branch, there are many different units that serve different types of missions in different situations. You will probably find that you have much in common with most other members of the U.S. military, but don't be surprised if your experiences don't always match exactly with those of your peers in other branches, units, or assignments.

WHO ARE THE NATION'S WARFIGHTERS?

In 2005 slightly more than 2.2 million individuals served in the U.S. military. Of these, 1.4 million served as active duty members of the U.S. Air Force, U.S. Army, U.S. Navy, and Marine Corps. The remainder (821,000) served as reservists through the U.S. Army National Guard, U.S. Army Reserve, U.S. Naval Reserve, U.S. Marine Corps Reserve, U.S. Air National Guard, and U.S. Air Force Reserve. New recruits numbered 154,000 assigned to active components and 110,000 assigned to reserve components.

In general, the largest percentage (41 percent) of new recruits comes from southern states. Since 1996, there has been an increase in the percentage of new recruits from western states and a corresponding decrease in the percentage of new recruits from northeastern states. Nearly half of all soldiers, sailors, Marines, and airmen are married. Among enlisted members, 50 percent of those on active duty and 47 percent of reservists are married. Military men are more likely to be married than military women. New recruits are less likely to be married than their civilian counterparts.

Members of the U.S. military are carefully screened, selected, and trained for a wide variety of occupations. People are sometimes surprised to learn that the military can be quite selective, and not all who volunteer are accepted. Each branch of service has its own needs and establishes its own standards and criteria for enlistment. Enlistment criteria are designed to ensure that individuals accepted for service are capable of performing general military duties. Applicants are screened on the basis of moral character, medical and physical fitness, level of education, and vocational aptitude test scores.

All branches of the U.S. military service use a single test (the Armed Services Vocational Aptitude Battery, or ASVAB) to help determine the enlistment eligibility of applicants. Scoring is done by reference to a nationally representative sample of 17- to 23-year-olds; for example, a score of 50 means that half of those sampled from the general population scored higher and half lower. At least 60 percent of all new recruits each year must score at or above the national average (50 or better).

In general, a high school diploma is the best single predictor of successful adjustment to military life. About 70 percent of high school graduates complete their first term of enlistment, compared to just half of those who did not graduate high school. Although the U.S. high school graduation rate is around 70 percent, the U.S. military currently requires that 90 percent of its members be high school graduates.

Moral-character enlistment standards are intended to minimize the enlistment of individuals who are likely to present serious disciplinary problems or security risks. Moral-character standards are designed to disqualify persons who have significant criminal records, a history of antisocial behavior, previous dishonorable military discharge, or other character traits that the U.S. military deems unsuitable for association with military personnel. No branch of the U.S. military permits the enlistment of individuals who are under any form of judicial restraint, such as bond, probation, imprisonment, or parole. Individuals who have been convicted of a single felony or of misdemeanors may receive a waiver to permit their enlistment, but waiver approval is based on a careful review of each case and is by no means automatic.

Physical and medical standards have been established to ensure that new recruits will be able to meet the physical requirements of basic training and military duties. Challenging job demands, harsh work environments, and potentially unavailable medications make it unreasonable to enlist individuals who suffer

Seabees assigned to the Naval Mobile Construction Battalion 3 at Camp Moreell, Kuwait. *U.S. Navy photo by Mass Communication Specialist 1st Class Carmichael Yepez*

from certain medical conditions (e.g., diabetes, asthma) that require the regular or frequent use of medications.

After all basic enlistment standards and screening measures have been applied and considered, the U.S. military counts within its membership a broad and diverse array of Americans from all corners of the nation and from all walks of life. Members of the U.S. armed forces represent majority and minority populations, single and married persons, men and women, and people of different faiths, sexual orientations, socioeconomic histories, and cultural and ethnic backgrounds.

A DIVERSE AND INTEGRATED MILITARY

The military is diverse in its membership and in its services. As in the past, changes in the composition of the U.S. military services have gradually come to reflect changes in the population and attitudes of American society as a whole. This section briefly reviews the integration of racial minorities, married persons, and women into the U.S. military, and it also discusses evolving issues surrounding the military service of gay and lesbian Americans.

RACIAL MINORITIES

In 1948, shortly after World War II, President Harry S. Truman signed an executive order to provide equal opportunity regardless of race in the armed forces. Although segregated units remained the norm for several more years, commanders observed successful integrated units in combat during the Korean War and announced formal plans to desegregate the Army in 1951. By 1954 the U.S. Army was a racially integrated force.

Today individuals of racial and ethnic minorities can be found in all areas of American military service. Many minority service members have risen to high enlisted and officer ranks. Notable examples include former chairman of the Joint Chiefs of Staff and former secretary of state Colin Powell, who in his military career rose to the rank of four-star general in the U.S. Army, and Luis Caldera, who graduated from the U.S. Military Academy at West Point and went on to become secretary of the Army.

Active and reserve military components are comparable in their representation of various racial and ethnic minorities. African Americans currently make up approximately 21 percent of those who serve within the broader age range (18–44 years) of the enlisted service members overall. This percentage is quite a bit higher than within the civilian population, where African Americans comprise 13 percent of the population. Roughly 15 percent of active duty recruits are African Americans; this is comparable to the percentage (14 percent) of African Americans among civilians in the same age group (18–24 years).

Across the total U.S. military force, Hispanics make up 10 percent of active duty enlisted members (versus 16 percent of the civilian population). Thirteen percent of active duty recruits describe themselves as Hispanic, compared to nearly 18 percent of civilians in the comparable age range (18–24 years). "Other" minorities (American Indians and Alaskan Natives, Asians, Native Hawaiians and Pacific Islanders, and those of two or more races) are represented in comparable proportion to their numbers in the civilian population, generally about 7 percent.

MARRIED SERVICE MEMBERS

Before the establishment of the all-volunteer force (AVF), marriage was less common in the military because most service members served for short durations. With the end of the draft—and with technological developments that made it necessary to retain skilled personnel for longer periods of time—married

Vice Chief of Staff of the Army Gen. Peter W. Chiarelli presents the Distinguished Service Cross to Staff Sgt. Christopher B. Waiters. *Photo courtesy of U.S. Army/Phil Sussman*

Airman 1st Class Jon Luna practices squad and fire team maneuvers. *U.S. Air Force photo/Tech Sgt. Scott T. Sturkol*

service members eventually became the norm. Today more than half of all service members are married, with rates slightly higher among active duty members (55 percent) than among those in the reserve component (51 percent). Military women are less likely than military men to be married. Of military women who are married, fully half are married to another service member. Overall, about 7 percent of active duty service members are in a "dual-military" marriage.

New recruits are less likely to be married than civilians of the same age, but enlisted personnel in the ranks E1–E4 are much more likely to be married and have children than civilians in the same age group. One consequence of this is that there are many military families with young spouses and children who may lack the maturity and experience to cope with the demands of military life. In response, the armed forces have established formal support services and programs to address needs for childcare, legal assistance, reunion and reintegration support after deployment, and training to strengthen social networks and self-reliance.

WOMEN IN THE MILITARY

Prior to 1970, women represented fewer than 2 percent of all U.S. military service members. Although women are still a minority population within the U.S.

Operations Specialist 2nd Class Ta'Shina Norfleet is welcomed home by her husband after a seven-month deployment. *U.S. Navy photo by Mass Communication Specialist 3rd Class Ricardo J. Reyes*

Students at the Center for Information Dominance Corry Station line up in formation. *U.S. Navy photo by Gary Nichols*

military, their representation has grown dramatically among the ranks of enlisted service members as well as officers. Approximately 17 percent of new active duty recruits are women, and women currently comprise 15 percent of enlisted service members on active duty. Fifteen percent of U.S. Army officers are women. In 2008 Gen. Ann E. Dunwoody became the first American woman to achieve the rank of four-star general. Women also comprise 17 percent of enlisted members in the selected reserve force and 22 percent of the overall selected reserve force. Among women serving as active enlisted members, 39 percent are also members of racial minority groups.

The U.S. military is a community in which men and women serve a variety of roles, some of which might be seen as nontraditional in the civilian world. In the military, it is not unusual to encounter men working as nurses and women working as mechanics. Here, men and women from all walks of life work together and depend on one another through stressful experiences such as field training, deployment, and combat. Women serve in combat roles on ships and aircraft. The U.S. Navy has indicated that it will soon allow its female members to serve on submarines.

Command Sgt. Maj. Teresa King takes over as commandant of the Drill Sergeant School, making her the first woman to hold the position. *Photo courtesy of the U.S. Army/Steve Reeves, Fort Jackson Leader*

Although military policy still formally excludes women from most ground combat assignments, in practice women are now routinely assigned to roles in units and situations where they are as likely as any other soldiers to be exposed to hostile action. Because today's battlefield has no clear front line, the traditional distinction between combat and noncombat service is often blurred. Military women work and fight side-by-side with military men and are just as likely to be captured, wounded, or killed. Women represent approximately 2 percent of all combat-related injuries and deaths in recent years, which is about ten times the percentage of servicewomen who were killed in World War II.

Military women have worked extremely hard to gain acceptance by their male peers. Men and women who have served in recent conflicts in Iraq and Afghanistan have seen firsthand that women can and do serve effectively in combat situations. In recent years two female soldiers—the first since World War II—have been awarded Silver Stars for their exceptional valor in combat in these conflicts.[1]

Women entering the military and military academies have sometimes en-countered resistance, harassment, and even violence. The military is concerned with the need to prevent sexual harassment and sexual assault against all service

Staff Sgt. Rosy Cueva, 25th Combat Aviation Brigade, prepares to fly with other members of her unit to sites throughout northern Iraq. *Photo courtesy of the U.S. Army*

Members of the 823rd Security Forces Squadron return from a six-month deployment to Iraq. *U.S. Air Force photo/Airman 1st Class Brittany Barker*

members. When you join the military, you will receive important training on these topics, along with every incoming recruit and every service member. Medical and religious personnel have been specially trained to counsel and provide assistance to victims of sexual harassment and assault. A new reporting system has also been established. Service members have the option to receive help without filing an official report. No form of sexual harassment or assault is acceptable in the military, and it will not be tolerated. A physical or verbal attack on any member of the U.S. military takes away from our readiness to fight and is an attack on the U.S. military itself.

GAY, LESBIAN, AND BISEXUAL WARFIGHTERS

Since 1993 gays, lesbians, and bisexual Americans have served legally in all branches of the U.S. military under a law known as "don't ask, don't tell." Under this law, there can be no questions ("don't ask") concerning the sexual orientation of a candidate, recruit, or service member. In exchange, service members are required to maintain their gay, lesbian, or bisexual sexual orientation as a purely private matter ("don't tell"). This means that gay, lesbian, and bisexual personnel are not allowed to mention their sexuality to anyone at any time while their service contract is in effect. Moreover, they must accept that homosexual behavior itself is prohibited.

The United States is part of the North Atlantic Treaty Organization (NATO) and has other formal treaties and alliances in place with other nations. This means that American forces will often be deployed to work and fight alongside military personnel from other countries. At least twenty-five nations currently do allow gay and lesbian military personnel to serve openly. Most of these are member nations of NATO, and many have fought alongside American forces in Iraq and Afghanistan.

For obvious reasons, it is difficult to address research questions in the course of active combat. And because gay and lesbian personnel cannot disclose their sexual orientation to anyone, it can be difficult to ascertain the psycho-

NATIONS ALLOWING GAYS TO SERVE OPENLY IN THE MILITARY	
Australia	Lithuania
Austria	Luxembourg
Belgium	Netherlands
Canada	New Zealand
Czech Republic	Norway
Denmark	Slovenia
Estonia	South Africa
Finland	Spain
France	Sweden
Germany	Switzerland
Ireland	United Kingdom
Israel	Uruguay

logical or performance impact of current law on those most directly affected by it until after they have left the military. Over the course of several decades, other questions about the possible impact of gay military service have been addressed by researchers from universities, independent agencies, and by members of the U.S. military itself.[2] Studies have been performed in the context of military training, by direct surveys of U.S. military personnel, by reference to the experiences of foreign militaries that allow open service, and in law enforcement and emergency response organizations where similar questions have been raised. Consistently, researchers have found and reported that openly gay service does not undermine military cohesion or overall readiness.

The experiences of foreign militaries also point to several important lessons about transition to open service. Research makes it clear that if the decision is made to allow open military service by gay men and lesbians, policy transition should be implemented quickly and with clear and decisive support from senior military leaders. These aspects of change are important to reduce uncertainty. It should also be clear that a single code of conduct applies to all military personnel and that commanders will discipline anyone who disobeys policy.

As we send this book to press, the future of "don't ask, don't tell" remains uncertain. The law has been successfully challenged in Federal District court, and the Pentagon has instructed military recruiters that they can now accept openly gay and lesbian recruits. Final resolution of legal challenges and appeals may take years. Repeal of "don't ask, don't tell" was included in the House of Representatives' version of the 2010 Defense Authorization bill, but the Senate version containing similar language was rejected by the full Senate a few months before the 2010 mid-term elections. The Department of Defense has, in the meantime, undertaken to survey service members and their families about possible repeal of "don't ask, don't tell" and has begun to plan for possible implementation of repeal. The Department has also made specific changes in enforcement of "don't aks, don't tell" until such time as the law itself is changed. For example, the use of overheard statements and hearsay will be discouraged as a basis for formal inquiry or separation proceedings. Discharge proceedings will no longer use information provided by service members to their lawyers, clergy, or psychotherapists. Information provided to physicians in the course of medical treatment or public health inquiry, and information provided for security clearance or professional assistance in domestic or physical abuse cases will also be excluded as evidence in discharge proceedings.

The experiences of other nations suggest that under similar conditions and behavior, a transition to open service is likely to be smooth and largely transparent to most service members. Until any change is made official, however, current law still provides for the discharge of any American service member who states that he or she is gay or bisexual, marries or attempts to marry someone of the same sex, or engages in homosexual conduct, which is defined as physical contact with someone of the same sex for the purpose of sexual gratification. The law applies to members of the U.S. military twenty-four hours a day, seven days a week, no matter where they are.

Although of course it is impossible to know precisely how many military personnel are gay, lesbian, or bisexual, analyses based on U.S. Census data suggest that these individuals may number around 65,000, or slightly more than 2 percent of active and reserve duty forces combined. Diverse as the U.S. military may be, all American service members are part of a unified military force, working and fighting together to defend the same great nation and its similarly diverse population. Your military service may also involve working with foreign military personnel whose cultures, traditions, laws, and regulations sometimes differ from our own. Successful teamwork requires sensitivity and tolerance to-

Crewman Qualification Training (CQT) students at Silver Strand beach in Coronado, California. CQT is a 14-week advanced training course for Special Warfare Combatant-craft Crewman (SWCC) trainees. SWCCs operate and maintain boats used to support Navy SEALS in special operations missions. *U.S. Navy photo by Mass Communication Specialist 2nd Class Christopher Menzie*

Guardsmen dash out of a building in pursuit of high-value targets during urban operations training. *Photo courtesy of the U.S. Army/Maj. Deanna Bague*

ward those who may be different, especially when those differences relate to deeply held beliefs or strong emotions.

TEAMWORK

Most military work is grounded in teamwork. It is always in your best interest to work well as a team member and promote teamwork among others in your unit, squad, platoon, or other working group. There are six basic, interrelated elements of teamwork: communication, cooperation, coordination, leadership, assertiveness, and planning. Usually, effective performance in one area will lead to effective performance in another. For example, good communication supports effective cooperation. These skills might seem obvious or sound easy, but they do not come naturally to most people. Don't be surprised if you have to work hard to improve your skills in many of these areas. It will be well worth your effort. Teams whose members practice the six elements of teamwork effectively are better able to accomplish their missions successfully, quickly, and with fewer problems.

COMMUNICATION

Good communication is essential to good teamwork. Successful communication occurs in three steps. First, you must express what you mean. Take care to explain ideas clearly, simply, and in sensible order. Second, the listener must check his or her understanding of the information you expressed. This second step is essential to preventing miscommunication. Finally, you must confirm or correct the listener's understanding. If it is necessary to provide correction, the listener should check again to be sure that the new information is clearly understood. Good communication should never be assumed. It never hurts to check or double-check your information. Miscommunication can cost lives and is often to blame for mission failure.

COOPERATION

By cooperative effort, people can do more in less time than they could do alone. If you didn't already know this, you probably learned it in boot camp. The value of cooperation applies to nearly every task you will do in the military, from filling sandbags to processing paperwork, from passing inspections to carrying out tactical missions. You don't have to like another person to cooperate with him or her. You simply have to recognize that mission success takes priority over personal feelings.

COORDINATION

Coordination is an extension of cooperation. Coordination refers to how well you (the team) use your time and resources. If you have multiple tasks to do, it might be important to do them in a sensible order to save time. Make sure the most essential tasks get done first so that subsequent tasks are not delayed.

At the same time, you should ensure that limited resources are used sensibly. Limited resources might include certain tools, computers, vehicles, or personnel with specialized skills. In some situations, it is best to avoid competition between tasks that require identical resources. In other situations, it may be possible to coordinate resources such that multiple tasks can be done at once.

LEADERSHIP

Everyone who serves in the military understands that leadership is important. Teams work best when they serve under effective leadership. Formal leadership—battalion commanders, company commanders, flight commanders, division officers, platoon leaders, element leaders, platoon sergeants, and squad leaders—make important decisions about how a mission should be accomplished and how resources will be used. You may also benefit from the informal leader-

Marines prepare gear for a convoy to Camp Al Taqaddum, Iraq. *U.S. Marine Corps photo/Cpl. Triah Pendracki*

ship of lower ranking team members who have important knowledge or experience for a particular task or mission. Good leaders will help develop leadership in others and recognize when others have unique knowledge or specific talents that can lead the team to success.

Assertiveness

Assertiveness refers to the ability to take initiative and speak up to provide information when you see that it is needed. If you see that someone has less information than they need or something is being done incorrectly, it is important that you speak up. Don't be shy. If you don't share information assertively, lives might be lost as a result. For example, in 1982, an Air Florida flight taking off in Washington, DC, crashed because the aircraft's wings had ice on them. Prior to takeoff, the copilot had observed that the de-icing equipment wasn't turned on and mentioned this problem to the pilot. The pilot disagreed. Rather than pressing the point, the copilot let it go. The plane then failed to generate adequate airspeed to take off and crashed into the Potomac River. All but six of the people on board were killed as a result. The co-pilot was correct in his original observation. Had he been more assertive, the tragedy could have been prevented.

Military service can be dangerous. Military personnel face risks not only in combat but also in training and in the course of their everyday service at home. Part of being a good teammate is being willing to speak up when you see that something is wrong, even if it means you might have to stop what you are doing to deal with the problem. Every member of the team should understand that it is better to spend a few minutes preventing a problem than to spend hours correcting it later. It is always worth the time and effort to ensure the safety of everyone on the team.

PLANNING

Planning is crucial to support coordination, communication, cooperation, and leadership. Planning provides the specific information that is needed for team members to know what to do—how, when, and with whom. Even simple tasks can be improved by planning.

Marines review an equipment offload plan at Camp Pendleton's Red Beach training area. *U.S. Marine Corps photo/LCpl. Megan Sindelar*

A plan doesn't have to be complicated or lengthy. A plan might be expressed very simply, such as, "I'll shovel, you hold the bags, and he'll tie them off, count them, and stack them. We'll switch off after every 20 bags." This plan provides structure and a basis for expectations. For more complex tasks, a plan should consider what resources and people will be needed, when and how people will have to communicate and work together, what decisions will have to be made in real time, and contingency plans for problems that might be encountered along the way. Ideally, every member of the team should be aware of the entire plan so that each individual knows what to expect and what is expected. A good plan should anticipate possible problems so that if something does go wrong, everyone on the team is prepared to act as a coordinated unit and move forward toward mission success.

You will find that the essential aspects of teamwork become easier after you have worked as a member of a team for some period of time. The more time people spend working together, the better they get at cooperating and communicating with one another. The process of teamwork becomes more efficient as team members get to know each other. With training and practice, you will get to know how your teammates respond to unexpected situations or difficulties. You will learn what your teammates mean when they say certain things or speak in particular ways. As people get to know one another and spend time together, they rely more on nonverbal communication and behavioral information. Coordination becomes more automatic, less effortful. There are many examples of this in sports, where team members seem to communicate almost without any visible cues at all. This is the result of much hard work, repetition, and practice. In the military, you get this hard work by training (e.g., battle drills), where you should take the opportunity to practice coordination with your teammates. Teams that have trained and worked together are typically more effective and more cohesive.

NEW TEAMMATES

When your team gets a new member, it is important to recognize the need for additional help and going back to basics. A new team member lacks the benefit of experience that comes with working together over time. He or she may need more explicit communication to understand what might seem obvious to everyone else. Unspoken coordination will put the new team member at a disadvantage, and this will hurt the team. Every existing team member has a

Two soldiers provide security while on a route reconnaissance mission exercise at the Joint Multinational Readiness Center. *Photo courtesy of the U.S. Army/Sgt. Kris A. Eglin*

responsibility to help the new team member learn about the team's procedures and priorities. Likewise, new team members should speak up when they realize they need more information. If old and new team members communicate openly with each other, new members will get up to speed quickly and the team's effectiveness will not suffer.

There may be times when you will have to integrate one or more teammates from outside your own branch of service. These might be individuals from another service branch, a different government agency, or another country. In each case, you should understand that more time and effort might be needed to communicate effectively.

People from other organizations might assume that you know or understand vocabulary, acronyms, or programs that are unfamiliar to you. Likewise, you may find that these individuals are unfamiliar with concepts that are fundamental to your everyday work. Coordination and planning should be done more carefully to ensure that everyone understands exactly what is going on. Remember that although communication may be more difficult at times, people from other services, agencies, and countries often bring new and valuable information and capabilities to benefit your mission. By making the extra effort necessary to integrate these individuals into your team, you can make your team more effective in the long run.

HOW WARFIGHTERS ARE MADE

The military is a training organization. When you first enter the military, you are required to complete intense basic and advanced training programs. After these initial training phases, much of your training will occur within your unit. The skills you learn may one day save your life or the lives of others. Active duty service members and reservists will return to formal training periodically throughout their careers to update these skills.

There are many modes of training and education in the military. Formal training usually occurs at an institution or school. You may also receive some of your training by distance learning (Internet). Of course, not everything you learn will be part of an organized course or program. You will also learn a great deal from your fellow service members. To help service members learn from one another, the U.S. military has developed Web-based professional forums (also known as knowledge networks or communities of practice) where service members can discuss topics of shared interest. The U.S. military has also organized a large amount of additional instructional information that can be accessed through service Internet portals. These portals are websites that provide links to useful information and tools. Through your service portal, you can find links to other military organizations, libraries, strategic planning documents, field manuals, and articles related to defense and national security issues published by newspapers around the world. New information and resources are added daily.

Each branch of service provides a system its members can use to record and manage their training experiences. These systems can be found through your service portal. They will enable you to identify and register for courses and keep a

Soldiers take part in an online Army leadership course available at Al Asad Air Base, Iraq. *U.S. Marine Corps photo/Lance Cpl. Jason Hernandez*

record of courses that you have completed. It is important that you monitor and maintain your training record so that you will register for the most appropriate training and receive proper credit for the training that you complete.

Finally, you may find it useful to visit your service branch's Center for Lessons Learned. Each center can be accessed via the Internet. There is also a Joint

Center for Lessons Learned. The mission of the centers is to gather information about past operations and provide an understanding of what went right and what went wrong. This information and perspective can be used to improve future operations. It is a useful way to learn from the experience of others.

FAMILY AND THE MILITARY LIFESTYLE

The military way of life places demands on service members and their families (including spouses, children, parents, and siblings). Family separations, frequent moves, and long and unpredictable work hours can be stressful for all concerned, and these demands require a high level of cooperation and coordination. Service members and their families often feel social pressure to conform to cultural military norms. Military service also entails the risk of injury and death, the fear of which service members and their families must learn to live with. Although it is impossible to anticipate all difficulties, adequate preparation can make the military lifestyle more gratifying and generally less stressful. Here, we will consider various ways in which military personnel and their family members can prepare themselves and improve their adjustment to military life.

Active duty military families are generally well supported by organizational branch and unit services. Many of these services and programs can now be accessed via the Internet. Your own military installation probably offers facilities such as libraries, Internet access, and programs to assist with financial management, emergency loans, counseling, childcare, new parent support services, and marriage enrichment. Within your assigned unit, you may find additional programs and services. For example, the Army has Family Readiness Groups (FRGs) to provide families with information about unit and installation services and to keep family members informed when their soldiers are deployed. These groups also enable family members to meet others with common interests and develop supportive relationships and friendships. FRGs are most active during deployments, but many units strive to maintain them throughout the deployment cycle. Programs such as Army Family Team Building (AFTB) also provide additional opportunities to learn the ins and outs of Army life in a supportive and friendly atmosphere.

Unfortunately, it is still the case that families living off post and families of reservists often find it more difficult to adjust to the stress of separations. These families tend to be more socially isolated, be less aware of support services, and have less access to them. During long deployments, reservists' families face unique challenges that can be stressful, such as transitioning from civilian health insurance to the military's health care system (TRICARE) or adjusting to changes in income when the reserve member must leave his or her civilian job to serve on active duty.

The U.S. military has undertaken special initiatives to promote support for reservists' families. Recognizing that reservists and their families typically do not live on or near major military installations, these programs and services are designed to go beyond the traditional installation-centered model of services. Instead, they take the form of active partnerships between the military and civilian providers, agencies, and community groups. Additional Internet-based services offer virtual support and assistance. (A list of helpful websites and services can be found in the Resources section at the end of this book.)

The Army National Guard maintains a network of more than 400 Family Assistance Centers (FACs) to assist military personnel and families in any service branch during periods of mobilization. FACs are dispersed in cities and towns throughout the United States. They offer assistance with military identification, TRICARE enrollment, deployment preparedness, and referrals.

FACs also provide a physical setting where family members who live off post can meet and interact with their peers to establish informal social networks. The U.S. National Guard Family Program website (www.guardfamily.org) provides additional information and programs for National Guard families.

Similarly, the U.S. Army Reserve Family Program provides special support for families of augmentees (military personnel who have been mobilized individually, rather than with their full unit). This service branch maintains a website (www.arfp.org) and staff to assist augmentees and their families with military benefits issues, communication during deployment, and access to civilian community support resources. USAR Family Program staff members maintain regular contact with families of augmentees throughout the service member's deployment.

Reservists and their families can also take advantage of online support resources such as Virtual Family Readiness Groups (VFRGs; www.armyfrg.org) and Military OneSource (www.militaryonesource.com; 1-800-342-9647). Military OneSource is a twenty-four-hour, seven-day-a-week information and referral service that is available worldwide to all members of the U.S. military members and their families. OneSource answers questions about military support resources, military benefits, deployment, moving, legal matters, parenting, childcare, career planning, education, money management, and other topics of interest to military members and their families. OneSource will also make arrangements to provide free, face-to-face counseling with professional civilian mental health care providers.

Military life sometimes involves prolonged separations from family and friends. This begins in training and will continue at various times throughout your military career. If you have always lived in close proximity to extended family (parents, siblings), you will have to adjust to separation from them as you are assigned to military duty stations around the country or overseas.

Some military duties such as sea duty, field training, military education, and deployment will force you to spend time away from your spouse and/or children. Most military families adjust well to these separations, and many find that their relationships grow deeper by working together to meet the challenge. It is important to seek support from friends and colleagues. Research in this area encourages specific strategies for easing the adjustment of separation, and the readjustment of returning home. Additional advice is available at www.military onesource.com.

While it is true that active duty military families are generally well supported by organizational branch and unit services, families that live off-post and families of reservists often find it more difficult to adjust to the stress of separations. These families tend to report more social isolation and less access to or awareness of support services. Special efforts can and should be made to support and help such families to locate and use available resources.

WHEN YOU GO AWAY

✓ Try to have a positive attitude. Stay informed. Avoid rumors.
✓ Make plans with flexibility. Expect changes in departure and return dates.
✓ Prepare legal affairs and financial matters in advance of separation.
✓ Make decisions together with your spouse and family. How will expenses be handled while you are away? Who will provide back-up childcare? Discuss possible problems and solutions in advance.
✓ Talk about how to maintain communication and trust during separation.
✓ Identify dependable and affordable communication strategies and services.
✓ Prepare audiotapes (voice, songs) and videotapes (stories) for your spouse and children to enjoy in your absence.
✓ Organize and exchange contact information with FRG leaders and volunteers, unit rear detachment, and key agencies and programs (e.g., Army Community Services, Family Support Center).
✓ Encourage and help your spouse to take advantage of available support programs and resources (e.g., FRG, Family Support Center).
✓ Communicate as often as possible while away. Prepare a list of things you want to talk about before you call. Provide reliable information to keep your family informed without unnecessary stress

Because military life involves frequent relocation, military families enjoy the opportunity to see and experience many new places and people. Of course, moving can also be a stressful experience. Relocation requires adjustment to new communities, climates, and regional customs. It is sometimes difficult for military spouses to find employment in a new location. The military offers services to support your transition to a new installation and its surrounding community. These services may include employment programs and sponsor programs through which other service members and their families can assist you in the effort to find housing and other necessary local resources. Ask about such services before you relocate. You may find that you can receive helpful assistance before you move.

Military work often requires that service members be available for duty twenty-four hours a day, seven days a week. Even when this requirement is not activated, there is the potential that it may be activated at any time. Moreover, routine duty at your home installation may involve long and sometimes unpredictable work hours. It is important that your family be made aware of this and that plans are made flexibly to adapt when necessary. Military families should always have routine back-up plans for transportation and childcare to accommodate last-minute changes that are unavoidable.

Military communities apply expectations for good behavior to service members and to their families. Spouses are expected to obey installation laws and rules. They may also feel some pressure to participate or volunteer in community and unit activities. Although participation in activities such as the unit FRG or Army Family Team Building is entirely voluntary, research suggests that involvement is helpful. Spouses who are involved in base activities are more informed and better able to build supportive relationships that help them to cope with life in the military.

Modern media includes round-the-clock coverage of im-

WHEN YOU RETURN HOME

- ✓ Expect that it will take time for family members to readjust. Expect that you will see changes in each other and in your relationship.
- ✓ Don't try to resume old roles immediately. Don't try to take back control of finances. Understand that your spouse and children have learned and accepted new responsibilities. Acknowledge and appreciate their efforts.
- ✓ Know that it will take time to resume your parenting relationship with children. Don't discipline them right away. They will need time to learn again to respond to you as a parent.
- ✓ You will probably need time to adjust to being back at home again. This is normal. Let your spouse know that this may take some time.

portant military operations. While it may be helpful to be generally well informed, it is not a good idea for family members to stay glued to the television during periods of deployment. Rumors are common during war, and media coverage tends to focus on sensational events. Friends and loved ones who spend too much time focused on popular media may suffer more stress than necessary. Military personnel and their families should be encouraged to seek reliable information from unit rear detachment commanders or FRG leaders who are well informed about specific units and their activities.

In spite of the many challenges posed by military family life, most service members and their families find a deep sense of reward and satisfaction in knowing that their lives contribute to the freedom and security of the nation. Those who educate themselves and draw upon available resources can turn challenges into opportunities for individual and family growth, self-sufficiency, and resilience.

CONCLUSION

The goal of this chapter was to provide a general orientation to military life and help you see yourself and your service within the larger context of military concerns and priorities. As a trained warfighter, you play an essential role as one individual among many who work together and who share a common sense of pride and commitment.

As you move ahead in your military career, you will gain the experience that is necessary to support a deeper understanding of your individual place and purpose within the military. In addition to experience, it is important that you seek knowledge to better understand yourself as a human being and as a warfighter. Such information is presented in other chapters of this book, where you will find information that may be vital to your understanding of warfighter performance and psychology.

CHAPTER TWO

Your Body and Your Mind

Your performance as a military professional depends first and foremost upon your ability to function as a human being. You probably don't think often about the many complex systems and processes by which your mind and body allow you to sense, perceive, and respond to the world around you. As long as you are healthy and functional, most of these essential processes and systems are hard-wired to do their work automatically. On a daily basis, your body does most of what you need it to do. It is easy to take for granted or even ignore the possibility that it might someday fail or mislead you.

To be the best warfighter you can be, you should have a basic understanding of how physical systems can affect how you think, what you feel, and how effectively you are able to do your job, make good decisions, and respond to stressful or demanding situations. For example, how your body responds to stress can have an enormous impact on your ability to perform otherwise simple job-related tasks. If you understand how and why this is true, you can anticipate and prevent potentially life-threatening mishaps on the battlefield.

The purpose of this chapter is to explain how basic physical processes related to sensory function, diet, sleep, and exercise can affect your performance on and off the battlefield. We will also address the impact of stress and what can be done to prevent or reduce damaging effects of stress. Finally, we will consider how harsh and extreme environments (heat, cold, high altitude) can affect your physical and mental abilities.

Keeping lookout after rushing and clearing a farmhouse during a simulated mission near Sahl Sinjar, Iraq. *U.S. Marine Corps photo/Lance Cpl. Jason Hernandez*

SENSATION AND PERFORMANCE

Human sensory systems are exquisitely sensitive even to subtle stimulation. The human eye can detect a candle flickering thirty miles away on a clear night. The human ear can register the ticking of a wristwatch twenty feet away in a quiet room. The human nose can identify a brief puff of cigarette smoke carried on the wind from a distant street corner. Human skin can detect even the slightest breeze. Depending on your situation and mindset, you may or may not be conscious of such subtle events in your environment. Armed with a basic knowledge of how your senses work, you can gain a better understanding of their power, limitations, and possible effects on your performance.

Vision

Of all the ways you gather information about the world around you, you depend most heavily upon your eyes. The pictures here show the front and side views of the human eye and also show how the lens of the eye focuses images on your retina. The lens is located just behind the pupil. Images are converted to electrical signals on the retina and then are carried to the brain by the optic nerve.

Light enters your eye and is focused by the cornea and lens to the back of the eye on the retina. The retina contains specialized nerve cells known as cones and rods. Cone receptors are sensitive to color. Rod receptors are sensitive to light intensity. When these cells are stimulated by light, they respond by transmitting electrical impulses to your brain, which interprets these complex visual electrical signals as images, movement, and orientation.

Although the human eye can detect a large variety of different colors, its sensitivity to color and brightness changes under different conditions. In daylight, the human eye relies primarily on photopic vision (mediated by cone cells) and is most sensitive to yellow colors. In darker conditions such as late evening and night, the human eye relies on scotopic vision (rod cells) and is most sensitive to blue-green colors. As a result, human beings are less able to distinguish between colors under conditions of relative darkness. This is something to consider as a practical limitation in the field. For example, you will typically find it more difficult to read colorful maps and charts after sunset.

If you are outside, your transition from photopic to scotopic vision will occur naturally and imperceptibly as darkness falls. However, if you suddenly move from daylight into a dark room, you will notice that it is difficult to adapt your vision. Adaptation to darkness via the shift to scotopic vision is an adap-

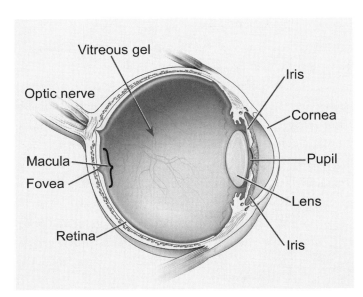

Diagram of the eye.
National Eye Institute, National Institutes of Health

tation process that takes approximately thirty minutes. One way to facilitate night vision is by the use of red light. Because the rod cells that support night vision are not sensitive to red, red light allows you to see without turning on bright lights or waiting for your eyes to fully adapt to darkness. This is why red lights are common as a form of illumination in darkened areas (e.g., sleeping quarters) and during night operations. Red filters are used on flashlights and many instrument panels are illuminated with red light for nighttime use. Your visual acuity is also good under red illumination, so red light can be used when you are reading a map.

There is one effect of darkness on the visual system that you have certainly experienced many times when viewing the night sky. In unobstructed darkness, a lone stationary object or point of light will appear to jerk, move, or jump around very suddenly. It can be a bit unsettling to perceive movement of an object that should not move (e.g., a star or a planet). Of course, the point of light itself is not moving. Its apparent movement is due to very small, very quick, imperceptible movements of the eye itself. Though we are usually unaware of these eye movements, they are normal and persistent.

As the eye moves, the image (in this case, the spot of light) is directed to different locations on the retina. When we have no other point of visual reference by which to judge the location of the image, our brains interpret this change as movement. It may be important to consider this phenomenon if you are assigned to monitor distant points of light at night.

Effects of high altitude. You should be aware that your ability to see and discriminate colors might deteriorate at moderately high altitudes (2,500–3,500 meters), even if you are fully acclimatized and working in daylight. This can affect mountaineers and aviators. Although the reason for reduced color sensitivity is not yet fully understood, it is a well-established phenomenon that is probably related to the effects of reduced oxygen supply to the retina. It is a common symptom of acute mountain sickness (AMS) experienced by mountain climbers.

Lasers and eye safety. Laser light is a unique form of coherent light delivered at a very specific wavelength. If the wavelength of the laser falls within the range of the light spectrum that is visible to the human eye, you will see it as an intense color. Laser light can travel long distances without losing power and poses potential hazards to the human eye. Laser light can be very intense. If viewed directly, it can cause damage to the cornea or to the retina. This danger exists even when laser light is delivered at wavelengths that are invisible to the human eye. It is important that you make yourself aware of laser sources that may be in use and never look directly at them. You should be especially cautious never to look directly at a laser source through binoculars or other vision magnification devices. This rule applies even to so-called eye-safe lasers such as those now commonly found in various types of commercial, law enforcement, and military equipment (e.g., grocery checkouts, laser pointers, Multiple Integrated Laser Engagement System training devices, rangefinders). Although Multiple Integrated Laser Engagement System (MILES) training devices are low-powered, they can pose a hazard if you intentionally look directly at the laser source at close range (less than ten meters). Always follow the standard operating procedures when you are training with, transporting, or performing maintenance on MILES devices.

HEARING

As a warfighter, you know the importance of your ability to hear. It is crucial that you be able to hear what is going on around you. You must be able to hear commands spoken by leaders and information delivered (sometimes in haste) by fellow soldiers. In order to perform effectively in combat, you count on your ability to detect vehicles, people, and potential threats. What you hear helps you

A member of the Combat Observation Laser Team sights out his target during a Fire Support Coordination Exercise. Photo Courtesy of the *U.S. Army/Pfc. Gregory Gieske*

define and interpret your surroundings. Your ears allow you to identify important changes in your environment. Sometimes, it is the absence of noise that alerts you to potential trouble.

The diagram shown here identifies various parts of the human ear. The outer ear ends at the eardrum. The middle ear contains three of the smallest bones in the human body. These transmit sound vibrations to the cochlea, which is the organ of hearing. The semicircular canals in the inner ear are necessary for balance and spatial awareness. The Eustachian tube connects the middle ear with the throat.

Sound waves are captured by your outer ears and then funneled within, where middle ear structures (eardrums and tiny bones) vibrate in response. These vibrations produce waves in the fluid-filled inner ear, which in turn create movement among tiny hair cells in the cochlea. The hair cells are receptors for sound. As they bend, they generate electrical signals that travel as nerve impulses to the brain. The brain then finally interprets these signals as sound.

Unfortunately, the tiny hair cells in the inner ear can be damaged by loud, intense noise. Damage can be caused by sudden and brief intense noise (e.g., gunshots) or by sustained intense noise (e.g., aircraft engines, jackhammers, loud

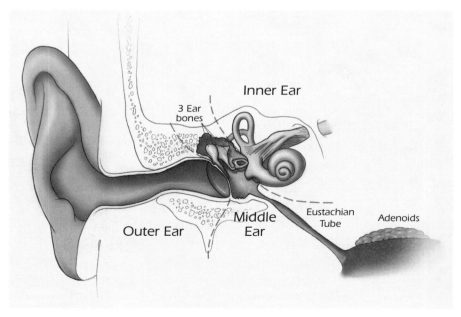

Anatomy of a normal ear. *National Institutes of Health*

music). Damage to hair cells can cause permanent loss of hearing at affected frequencies. The intensity, or volume, of sound is measured on the logarithmic decibel (dB) scale. For example, the sound of a whisper is measured at approximately 20 dB, normal conversation at around 60 dB, heavy traffic at 90 dB, power equipment at 90–100 dB, jackhammers and other impact equipment at 115 dB, indoor rock concerts at 120 dB, and airplane engines at 120–140 dB. Intensities above 120 dB are usually painful to hear.

Helmets for crew wear on military vehicles have integrated hearing protection. Passengers, however, must provide their own protection. Foam earplugs are very effective but tend to muffle speech and hinder the detection of low-frequency noises, so they are a problem in combat operations. The Army has developed a Combat Arms Earplug that can be used in both continuous and impulse noise situations. Learn how to use them correctly and always carry them with you.

Work environments that involve sustained noises above 85 dB can cause permanent hearing damage. If you spend just a few hours in noise above 85 or 90 dB, you may experience temporary but measurable loss of hearing sensitivity. Many people do not realize that the use of portable headphone music devices (e.g., audio tape, DVD, and MP3 players) can be dangerous because it is easy to

TABLE 2.1

Noise Levels	dB
Continuous	
HMMWV (30 mph)	84
Forklift/warehouse operations	85
Tactical "quiet" generators	80–87
HMMWV (55 mph)	94
Aircraft Carrier, Galley Deck (during flight operations)	100
Blackhawk helicopter (pilot seat)	106
M1A2 Abrams tank (30 mph)	114
Bradley Fighting Vehicle (20 mph)	115
Aircraft Carrier, Flight Deck	145
Impulse	
M16 rifle, M9 pistol	157
LAW, TOW II, 82 mm mortar	178–182

Lt. Cmdr. Paul Treadway uses a sound level meter to demonstrate the high decibel levels on the USS Abraham Lincoln's flag bridge. Safety personnel ensure sailors and workers are wearing proper personal protective equipment to protect against industrial hazards such as high noise levels. *U.S. Navy photo by Mass Communication Specialist Seaman James R. Evans*

increase their sound volume to potentially damaging levels without discomfort. A good rule of thumb for usage of these devices is that if others around you can also hear the music while you are wearing headphones, the volume is too high and could cause damage to your hearing.

The pitch, or frequency, of a sound is commonly measured in hertz (Hz), which refers to the number of "cycles per second" of the sound wave. The normal human ear can detect a wide range of frequencies from as low as 20 Hz (e.g., the sound of a low-pitched pipe organ) to as high as 20,000 Hz (e.g., whistles and even some cell phone ring tones). However, extreme frequencies in this range are relatively rare in the course of everyday life. In general, human hearing is most sensitive to frequencies between 2,000 and 4,000 Hz, which is the typical range of frequencies for spoken words. At these frequencies, a sensitivity loss of as little as 20 dB can make it difficult to understand human speech.

As we age, we naturally lose some sensitivity in our hearing. This change affects higher frequencies first, followed by a gradual loss of progressively lower frequencies. Eventually, we begin to notice that it is more difficult to understand speech in person or otherwise (by radio, television, telephone). Human hearing can also be temporarily or permanently damaged by disease or by the use of medications, including certain antibiotics (aminoglycoside), chemotherapy drugs, anesthetics, cardiac drugs, mood altering drugs (e.g., tricyclic antidepressants), cortisone, and steroids.

SMELL AND TASTE

Smell and taste are the result of a complex interplay between receptor cells and the brain. Smell and taste are now classified as chemical senses because they occur in response to chemicals that are present in the air or in solution. Both of these senses involve specialized nerve cell receptors located in the nose, tongue, and mouth. It is not known how many different and complex scents the human nose can detect and distinguish. One classification system identifies six general categories of odors: fragrant (e.g., flowers), spicy (e.g., cloves, nutmeg), ethereal (e.g., oranges), resinous (e.g., solvents such as turpentine), putrid (e.g., rotten eggs), and burnt (e.g., asphalt or tar).

Traditionally, it has been known that the human tongue can identify and distinguish among four different tastes: sweet, sour, salty, and bitter. A fifth taste known as "umami" has also been identified to describe the savory or meaty taste that is commonly associated with Asian foods.

Individuals can differ in their ability to distinguish odors and tastes. This may explain some personal preferences for certain foods and environmental surroundings. Some individual differences are quite dramatic. For example, some people (about 1 percent) cannot detect the smell associated with a skunk. Although differences in the ability to smell or taste usually have little practical impact on human performance or survival, there are situations in which these senses may play an important role. For example, smell and taste can detect spoiled food, the presence of diesel fuel, or smoke.

OTHER IMPORTANT SENSES

In addition to vision, hearing, smell, taste, and touch, your body has senses that provide you with additional knowledge of your environment and your body's place within it. We usually don't think about these other senses until they alert us to something uncomfortable or potentially dangerous:

Chemical senses (via taste and/or smell)
Cutaneous senses (e.g., touch, pressure, heat, cold, pain)
Kinesthesis (movement of limbs)
Proprioception (position of limbs)
Vestibular (balance and orientation)

Full awareness of your body and your surroundings depends upon your ability to sense touch, pressure, heat, cold, moisture, body orientation, position, and pain. All of these senses can be essential to human performance and have obvious adaptive and survival value.

Virtually all types of physical movements and tasks require kinesthesis, proprioception, and vestibular sensation. A mismatch between visual and vestibular information can cause motion sickness. Darkness can cause disorientation. In some military environments, vestibular sensation can be fooled with disastrous results. For example, nighttime aviation and underwater operations can challenge one's ability to sense balance and orientation. Countless aircraft accidents have been attributed to pilots' loss of orientation.

All of our senses are important, and deficits or disruptions of any kind can have severe con-

---

BALANCING ACT

Your eyes and inner ears work together to help you maintain your balance.

Try this quick demonstration with a friend:

Ask your friend to stand and look straight ahead with both eyes open and extending both arms.

Now ask your friend to raise one foot up off the ground and keep his or her balance by standing only on the other foot. (Most people can do this without much difficulty.)

After a few seconds, ask your friend to close his or her eyes. (After a second or two, your friend may begin to wobble a bit.)

Next, ask your friend to stand again on both feet, arms lowered, with eyes still closed. Place your hands on his or her shoulders and carefully turn your friend around five or six times.

Now, again ask your friend to stand on one foot again, eyes closed and with both arms extended. At this point, your friend will probably feel very unbalanced. (Provide support if necessary to prevent a fall or injury.)

Tell your friend to open his or her eyes to see if balance improves.

This demonstration shows how important your eyes and inner ears are to maintaining balance. Even a moment or two of visual distraction or physical disorientation can interfere with your situational awareness in a critical moment.

sequences for military performance and survival. If you sustain permanent sensory damage, you will have to live with that loss for the rest of your life. When basic protective equipment is available, you should use it. Laser vision goggles, sunglasses, ballistic eye protection, earplugs, and talk-through earphones are essential to your current safety and future well-being. Although they may seem cumbersome at times, by wearing and using them when needed, you will adjust to operating efficiently while protecting the critical sensory organs and functions of your body.

EAT WELL, LIVE LONG

Your body needs food to create energy for activity and health. Foods provide three primary nutrients (macronutrients) and various other essential vitamins and minerals (micronutrients). Macronutrients are carbohydrates, proteins, and fats; these are in nearly every food we eat. In this respect, there is no such thing as bad food. The more important question is how much you eat of any particular type of food and how often. If your diet is high in fat and calories, you are probably not getting many of the essential vitamins, minerals, and dietary fiber found in fruits and vegetables.

Different types of food contain different levels of macronutrients. As a general rule, it is recommended that we consume 50–60 percent of our caloric intake as carbohydrates, 15 percent as protein, and 25–35 percent as fat. Whether or not you track your caloric intake by source, three basic concepts should guide your eating habits: variety, balance, and moderation.

A healthy diet includes a variety of foods from each of the five main food groups on a daily basis:

Grains (breads, cereal, rice, and pasta)
Fruits
Vegetables
Meats (includes fish, beans, eggs, and nuts)
Dairy (includes milk, yogurt, and cheese)
Fats, oils, and sweets are sometimes listed as an additional separate food group but should be limited to small amounts.

By eating a balanced daily diet, you can ensure that your body receives the proper amounts of carbohydrate, protein, fat, and other essential vitamins and minerals. (Special considerations concerning food and nutrient supplements are discussed later in this section.) There are several easy ways to make sure you are eating properly. One helpful strategy is to make your meals colorful by including meat with vegetables, salad, rice, and fruit. Rather than eating processed snack foods such as cookies and chips (high in refined sugar and fat), snack on fruits, nuts, or vegetables. Dried fruits such as raisins are easy to carry and consume. Dry roasted nuts are much healthier for you than potato chips. Concerning fruits and vegetables, nutritionists recommend that you "strive for five," meaning that you should try to consume five servings of these foods each day. A serving may be smaller than you think. One apple or a handful of raisins counts as a full serving of fruit.

One important and effective way to maintain a healthy diet and control your weight is to limit portion size. Never super size your meal at a fast food restaurant. Remember, too, that restaurants in general tend to serve food and beverages in unnecessarily large portions. When you eat out, or if you frequently purchase prepackaged food, you can easily consume hundreds of unneeded or empty calories such as those found in sugared soft drinks.

EATING IN THE FIELD

In a garrison environment (fixed base or permanent facilities), military dining services are well suited to provide nutritious, well-balanced meals and proper portions. Service members themselves also have a personal responsibility to make good and healthy choices from among available foods. Remember that although high-fat, high-calorie foods may sometimes appeal to you, they are not beneficial to your health in the long run.

Military operations and field duty environments pose unique challenges to proper nutrition. Military personnel who work in these conditions need to consume more calories because they are typically more active than they would be in garrison. However, for obvious reasons, it can be difficult to prepare fresh food and hot meals in the field. Basic individual field rations—Meals Ready to Eat (MRE)s—have been designed and undergo constant improvement to address these difficulties. An

---

ABOUT MREs

A scientific study was performed to determine the effectiveness of MREs. Marine engineers ate only MREs for thirty consecutive days while building an airfield. The results of this study demonstrated that MREs are healthy and effective in providing adequate calories for labor-intensive field operations.

A squad leader enjoys a few moments of down time along with the rest of his squad as they break open their MREs while taking cover in a burned out hotel in Haqlaniyah. *U.S. Marine Corps/CPL Jan M. Bender*

MRE is a highly engineered set of foods designed and issued to provide adequate nutrition and calorie intake in austere environments. Each complete MRE packet provides about 1,300 calories (16 percent protein, 24 percent fat, 60 percent carbohydrates). The supplemental pouch bread provides an additional 200 calories. Eaten daily, three MREs will provide sufficient caloric intake for personnel who operate in active field environments. MREs also provide a proper amount of macronutrients, vitamins, and minerals.

Unfortunately, after several days, MREs can become monotonous and unappealing. To overcome this problem, new editions of MREs include a greater variety of entrees, spices, brand-name commercial products, and more ethnically diverse choices. Because sets of foods are packaged together in MREs, personal preferences may be difficult to satisfy. It is common for soldiers to trade food items. However, you should not make a habit of eating only one or two items from an MRE packet. Items are packed together to ensure that you receive the proper nutritional balance of protein, fats, and carbohydrates. If you repetitively eat only a few of the packaged items, you will upset that balance.

Research shows that how much we eat may be influenced by social factors such as eating with others in a group. You will probably eat better if you sit and eat with friends or members of your unit. Although this may be difficult to achieve in some operational settings, leaders should be aware of the benefits and do as much as possible to create as conducive an environment as the mission permits. Finally, food consumption is influenced by the availability of water and other drinks. Simply providing larger cups for dispensing beverages can increase food consumption.

Eating for Good Performance in Extreme Environments

In general, there are no special requirements for eating to support operations and activities in extreme environments. Scientific studies have not identified the need to change what types of foods we eat or vitamins and minerals we consume when we work in extreme heat, cold, or at high altitudes. Currently available rations are adequate for physically demanding operations in all climates.

Extreme environments do present some unique concerns, however. For example, the human body expends more energy to keep itself warm in cold environments. For this reason, special cold weather rations have been designed to provide additional calories to support increased energy expenditure. Cold weather rations provide approximately 4,500 calories per day (versus approximately 3,900 calories for regular rations), which is sufficient to support the need for additional energy in cold operational settings. You should also be aware that at high altitudes, you will have less appetite for food. Coupled with the need for greater energy due to cold or operational workload, this can lead to unwanted weight loss. If you find yourself working in any extreme environment, you should pay very close attention to your eating habits and ensure that you are consuming food as needed to support adequate caloric intake and nutrition.

It is essential to consume an adequate amount of water in all environments, particularly those that involve extreme heat and/or physical workload. Dehydration in hot environments can lead to heat exhaustion and heat stroke. How much water your body needs to avoid dehydration will change depending on your environment and your workload. Table 2.2 provides a good guide to maintaining adequate hydration in warm weather under various continuous workload conditions.

Dietary Supplements

So-called performance-enhancing food and nutrients are now frequently advertised to improve strength and/or endurance. These products are usually designed

TABLE 2.2

Water Intake (quarts per hour)			
Temperature	Easy Work	Moderate Work	Hard Work
<90 degrees F	0.5	0.75	0.75–1
>90 degrees F	0.75–1	1	1

Easy Work: Duties in garrison, marksmanship training
Moderate Work: Aerobic exercise, marching, calisthenics
Hard Work: Marches with heavy loads, assaults, extended aerobic exercise

and intended to improve the performance of elite athletes and body builders. They include electrolyte replacement drinks (e.g., Gatorade), energy drinks, specially formulated power bars, specific amino acid and other nutritional supplements, steroids, growth hormone releasers, stimulants (caffeine, amphetamine, ephedrine), and many others too numerous to mention. When considering the use of these supplementary products, bear in mind that the physical and mental requirements of the military operational environment are not identical to those of elite athletic competitions. You should be cautious about the advertised benefits of such products and carefully consider whether their advertised benefits would apply to your own needs in a military field operation. Be careful not to confuse drinks that replace electrolytes, water, and other nutrients (sports drinks) with so-called energy drinks containing caffeine and simple sugars. Sports drinks are isotonic, which means that they replace electrolytes in proportion to what you lose through sweating. Isotonic drinks are beneficial for extended work periods in hot weather.

Electrolyte supplements. When you sweat, your body loses electrolytes, which are minerals (e.g., sodium, potassium, calcium, magnesium) that regulate bodily functions. It is beneficial to replace electrolytes that are lost during high-workload tasks or missions that last more than an hour or two. Sports drinks (like Gatorade) can be good but are difficult to carry in the field and may not taste good unless refrigerated. Because commercial products are generally unavailable, Marines sometimes use a lightly salted water solution. These solutions are prepared under the supervision of medical and field hygiene personnel and should not be attempted by individuals without proper guidance. A simpler way to replace lost electrolytes is to eat small salted snacks such as pretzels or salted nuts, salt your food at mealtime, and consume extra water.

Table 2.3 shows an isotonic fluid replacement drink (left) versus an energy drink (right). The fluid replacement drink will replace electrolytes lost due to sweating during high work outputs. The energy drink provides calories drawn from simple sugars. Simple sugars and caffeine can provide a quick boost, but they do not support sustained performance.

Carbohydrate supplements. Energy drinks are designed to provide additional calories as well as fluid replacement. Many commercial products should be avoided because they contain lots of sugar and caffeine. However, the military has developed a number of better products (HooAH Bars, ERGO drinks, Energy Gels) that do provide sustained energy. Studies with elite military units have shown that properly formulated energy drinks can enhance performance and make a tactical difference. Make sure your energy drink contains complex carbohydrates such as maltodextrine and that it does not contain only fructose or corn syrup. Complex carbohydrates are absorbed more slowly, which allows a more controlled delivery of glucose to the body.

Simple sugars such as those found in most candy bars are absorbed very quickly, which causes a large, sudden increase in blood glucose followed by a

TABLE 2.3
COMPARISON OF FLUID REPLACEMENT (SPORTS) DRINKS AND ENERGY DRINKS

Fluid Replacement (Sports) Drink	Energy Drink
Nutrition Facts Serving Size 8 fl oz (240 mL) Servings Per Container 4 **Amount Per Serving** **Calories** 50 % Daily Value* **Total Fat** 0g — 0% **Sodium** 110mg — 5% **Potassium** 30mg — 1% **Total Carbohydrate** 14g — 5% Sugars 14g **Protein** 0g *Percent Daily Values are based on a 2,000 calorie diet.	**Nutrition Facts** Serving Size 1 Can Amount Per Serving: Calories 110 % Daily Value* Total Fat 0g — 0% Sodium 200 mg — 8% Total Carb. 28g — 9% Sugars 27g Protein less than 1g Niacin 100% • Vitamin B6 250% Vitamin B12 80% • Pantothenic Acid 50% Not a significant source of sat. fat, trans fat, cholest., fiber, vitamin A, vitamin C, calcium and iron. 2,000 calorie diet.
Water, Sucrose Syrup, High Fructose Corn Syrup (Glucose-Fructose Syrup), Citric Acid, Natural and Artificial Flavors, Salt, Sodium Citrate, Monopotassium Phosphate, Glycerol Ester of Wood Rosin, Sucrose Acetate Isobutyrate, Yellow 5.	Carbonated Water, Sucrose, Glucose, Sodium Citrate, Taurine, Glucuronolactone, Caffeine, Inositol, Niacinamide, Calcium-Pantothenate, Pyridoxine HCL, Vitamin B12, Natural and Artificial Flavors, Colors.

dramatic drop in blood glucose. Properly made nutrition bars will not cause this problem if they contain complex carbohydrates and a balanced inclusion of some fat, protein, and dietary fiber. It is important that you remember to drink extra water when you consume carbohydrate supplements of any kind.

Table 2.4 below compares a nutrition bar (first) with a typical candy bar (bottom). The candy bar provides 35 percent of its calories from fat and has a large amount of

ERGO

During an intense 9-hour exercise, elite American soldiers were given multiple portions of the energy drink ERGO. The exercise involved intense aerobic activities, including a 12-mile forced march, two 3-mile runs, and a live-fire exercise.

Soldiers who used the ERGO drink had significantly faster run times on the second 3-mile run than those who had consumed only water throughout the exercise.

The group of soldiers that performed best was the group whose members had received a total of 300 grams of carbohydrates over the course of the 9-hour exercise. Some benefit was also seen in the group whose members had received a total of 150 grams of carbohydrates in their drinks.

simple sugars, little fiber, and almost no protein or other nutrients. The nutrition bar provides only 20 percent of its calories from fat and is a source of protein, fiber, and essential nutrients. Knowing this difference can help you make smart choices about the foods you select in times of intense physical activity.

Amino acids. Supplemental intake of specific amino acids is generally ineffective in producing significant benefits and can even be dangerous. These products are largely unregulated and can cause toxic side effects or undesirable interactions with certain medications. With these cautionary notes in mind, it

ERGO (Energy Rich Glucose Optimized) is a powdered drink that comes in orange, lemon, lemon-lime, raspberry, and tropical punch flavors. Mixed with 12 ounces of water, one serving delivers 170 calories. *U.S. Department of Defense*

The Hooah! bar is a carbohydrate-rich food item meant to help sustain a high energy level on the battle-field. *U.S. Department of Defense/Phil Copeland*

can be said that some supplements of this type may be useful. Aspartic acid may be effective in improving endurance tasks, but this has been demonstrated only in well-controlled laboratory settings. Creatine is marketed to increase muscle mass and may improve performance on tasks that require bursts of strength or energy (e.g., sprinting). Although it is doubtful that creatine actually increases muscle mass, there is now evidence from laboratory research and field studies to show that it can have a significant beneficial effect on performance when it has been taken consistently for five to six days prior. Tyrosine is a compound that is used by the body to produce important neurotransmitters used by the body and in the brain. Extra dietary tyrosine has not been shown to improve physical performance but may be beneficial to withstanding the mental stresses of operations in extremely cold environments. Several other amino acids (e.g., arginine, glycine, ornithine) have been marketed to promote the release of growth hormone as a means to stimulate muscle mass and improve strength. However, it is unlikely that any of these products can produce a release of growth hormone that has any physical significance or performance benefit.

Vitamins and minerals. Over the course of a lifetime, it is valuable to consume the recommended daily amounts of micronutrients (vitamins and miner-

TABLE 2.4

NUTRITION BAR AND CANDY BAR INGREDIENTS AND NUTRITIONAL VALUES

Nutrition Bar

Nutrition Facts

Serving Size 1 bar (50g)

Calories 210
 Calories from Fat 60

*Percent Daily Values (DV) are based on a 2,000 calorie diet.

Amount/serving	% DV*	Amount/serving	% DV*
Total Fat 7g	11%	**Potassium** 120mg	3%
Saturated Fat 4g	20%	**Total Carbohydrate** 24g	8%
Trans Fat 0g		Dietary Fiber <1g	2%
Cholesterol <5mg	1%	Sugars 16g	
Sodium 150mg	6%	**Protein** 13g	25%

Vitamin A	50% • Vitamin C	100% • Calcium	10% • Iron	25% • Vitamin E	100% • Vitamin K	25%
Thiamin	25% • Riboflavin	25% • Niacin	25% • Vitamin B6	25% • Folic Acid	25% • Vitamin B12	25%
Biotin	25% • Pantothenic Acid	25% • Phosphorus	15% • Iodine	25% • Magnesium	10% • Zinc	25%
Selenium	25% • Copper	25% • Manganese	25% • Chromium	25% • Molybdenum	25%	

Ingredients: Balance Pro 4 Protein Blend (Casein Whey Protein Isolate, Partially Hydrolyzed Casein and Whey Soy Protein Isolate), Sugar, Corn Syrup, Evaporated Cane Juice Invert Syrup, Glycerin, Fractionated Vegetable Oil, (Palm and Palm Kernel Oils), High Maltose Corn Syrup, Peanut Butter (Roasted Ground Peanuts), Nonfat Milk, Cocoa (Processed With Alkali), Contains Less Than 2% of Natural Flavor, Milk, Whey Protein Concentrate, Fractionated Palm Kernel Oil, Canola Oil, Heavy Cream, Maltodextrin, Maltitol Syrup, Peanut Flour, Fructose, Peanut Oil, Soy Lecithin, Salt, Butter, (Cream, Salt, Annato For Color), Partially Defatted Peanut Flour, Sodium Caseinate, Carrageenan, Fish Gelatin, Mixed Tocopherols (To Help Protect Flavor).

Candy Bar

Nutrition Facts

Serving Size 10 blocks (40 g)
Servings Per Container about 3

Calories 210
 Calories from Fat 110

*Percent Daily Values (DV) are based on a 2,000 calorie diet.

Amount/Serving	%DV*	Amount/Serving	%DV*
Total Fat 12 g	18%	**Total Carb.** 24 g	8%
Sat. Fat 7 g	35%	Dietary Fiber < 1 g	3%
Trans Fat 0 g		Sugars 23 g	
Cholesterol 10 mg	3%	**Protein** 3 g	
Sodium 40 mg	2%		

Vitamin A 2% • Vitamin C 0% • Calcium 8% • Iron 2%

Ingredients: Milk Chocolate (Sugar; Milk; Cocoa Butter; Chocolate; Lactose; Soy Lecithin; PGPR, Emulsifier; Natural and Artificial Flavor).

als) to maintain good health. It is probably not a bad idea to take a daily multivitamin supplement, especially if you find yourself unable to maintain a healthy, well-balanced diet. However, there is no substitute for good nutrition. If you eat a normal diet that includes the recommended servings of fruits and vegetables, you will have already consumed adequate amounts of these and other vitamins. You should consult with a physician before adding vitamin or mineral supplements to your daily diet. Certain vitamin and mineral supplements might interfere with the effectiveness of others (e.g., calcium interferes with the absorption of fluoride) or with the absorption of specific medications (e.g., iron interferes with absorption of thyroid hormone).

You should also be aware that short-term increases in the intake of any particular vitamin or mineral will not have any noticeable effect on your operational performance. Except when used to prevent or reverse specific vitamin-deficient diseases that are rarely seen in modern industrialized societies, vitamins and minerals have not been proven useful as a short-term strategy to improve normal performance in otherwise healthy young adults. While some research suggests that vitamins C and E (antioxidants) can reduce muscle soreness, improve wound healing, and prevent

> **THINGS YOU SHOULD NOT DO**
>
> ✓ DO NOT take excess amounts of vitamin or mineral supplements.
> ✓ DO NOT use steroids to enhance strength or performance.
> ✓ NEVER combine caffeine and ephedrine!
> ✓ NEVER use controlled substances such as amphetamines without medical orders!

infections, other studies challenge these findings. In general, you should avoid excess consumption of any vitamin or mineral supplement.

Stimulants. The use of caffeine (found in coffee, cola, chocolate, and other products) is quite common. Caffeine exerts direct alerting and arousal effects and has been shown to be effective in improving aerobic endurance, possibly as the result of changes in energy metabolism. Caffeine may also be of some benefit to anaerobic capacity and muscular endurance. The benefits of caffeine are greatest for people who do not use it on a regular basis or who use it after having restricted their regular use of it for several days prior. Caffeine is sometimes used in combination with ephedrine (also known as ephedra), which is a stimulant that is found in herbal medications. Ephedrine is related to the common decongestant medication pseudoephedrine. Although the combination of caffeine and ephedrine does have a significant positive effect on aerobic capacity in some sports (e.g., cycling and running), it has been banned from athletic competitions and *should never be used* because it can also produce dangerous increases in blood pressure and heart rate. Finally, pharmaceutical stimulants such as amphetamine and modafinil (Provigil) are controlled substances and should *never be used without medical orders*. These drugs are not prescribed for the purpose of enhancing performance.

Steroids. If you follow professional sports and athletic competition, you probably know about the abuse and hazards associated with steroids. Despite their dangers, these compounds are used frequently among athletes who are willing to sacrifice their health to gain a competitive edge on their opponents. It is known that the long-term use of steroids leads to increased muscle mass, but the extent and impact of this effect has not been rigorously studied in normal adults. Steroid use can also produce significant negative physical, psychological, and emotional effects, including severe acne, shrinkage of the testes, reduced sperm count, masculinization in women, increased aggressiveness, and outbursts of rage. Simply put, you should never use steroids in an effort to enhance your strength or performance. Steroids do more harm than good and may in fact do no appreciable good at all.

FITNESS AND EXERCISE

There are two important reasons for you to exercise and maintain your physical fitness. Regular exercise will keep you healthy and enable you to do your job. You should include physical exercise as part of your daily routine. The purpose of a regular exercise program is to build and maintain four essential components of physical fitness.

Cardiovascular health and aerobic capacity. Aerobic capacity refers to your ability to perform at a high heart rate over an extended period of time. Aerobic capacity is important in activities such as running, swimming, and bicycling, and in sports such as soccer and lacrosse. In fact, military fitness tests employ activities such as running, biking, or swimming to measure aerobic fitness. To improve your aerobic capacity, cardiovascular exercises should be performed for at least thirty minutes at an intensity that increases your heart rate to between 65 percent and 80 percent of your age-adjusted maximal heart rate, which is calculated as follows:

Men: 220 - your age (in years) = age-adjusted max heart rate
(*Example:* If you are a 25-year-old man, your age-adjusted maximal heart rate is 195 beats per minute. Therefore, your target heart rate during exercise should be between 127 and 156 beats per minute.)

Women: 226 - your age (in years) = age-adjusted max heart rate
(*Example:* If you are a 25-year-old woman, your age-adjusted maximal heart rate is 201 beats per minute. Therefore, your target heart rate during exercise should be between 131 and 161 beats per minute.)

Your heart is a muscle. When you exercise your heart, it grows larger and stronger. Regular aerobic exercise improves your heart's ability to pump blood and thus deliver oxygen to muscles throughout your body. A program of regular aerobic exercise not only strengthens your heart but can also significantly improve your body's ability to utilize oxygen. With regular aerobic exercise, the mitochondria in your muscle cells (which produce energy) grow larger and more numerous. This allows your muscles to work harder and longer without fatigue. Aerobic capacity is measured in laboratories with specialized tests such as a treadmill VO_2 max test. This test measures the maximum amount of oxygen your body can use per unit of time.

Members of the mobilized reserve unit Maritime Expeditionary Command and Control Division 24 sprint during the run portion of the Marine Corps Combat Fitness Test. *U.S. Navy photo by Mass Communication Specialist Maddelin Angebrand*

Muscular strength. Strength refers to your muscles' ability to work against resistance, such as when you lift heavy objects. Strong muscles are less likely to suffer injury under high workload. To build and maintain muscle strength, you should perform a regular and progressive program of resistance training with weights.

It is important to remember that weight training should be done by gradual incremental increases in weight. Sudden, dramatic increases in the amount of weight resistance can cause serious injury to your muscles, joints, and back.

Muscular endurance. Endurance refers to your muscles' ability to perform a sustained amount of work for an extended period of time. You can improve your muscular endurance capacity by performing regular simple and repetitive physical exercises such as push-ups and sit-ups.

Flexibility. It is important that your body be able to bend and stretch without injury. The more physically flexible you are, the less likely it is you will suffer injuries such as torn ligaments or tendons during demanding physical exercises or tasks. To improve flexibility, practice careful warm-up stretching before and after aerobic exercise or activity. Always begin stretching within a small range of motion, gradually increasing your range over multiple repetitions. Never "bounce" or use "explosive" motions to warm up. If you wish to improve your flexibility in particular, focused activities such as yoga can be especially helpful.

Weight control and health. Different types of physical activity require different amounts, ratios, or percentages of protein, carbohydrates, and fat. This is why a comprehensive exercise program should include activities for all major components of fitness (aerobic capacity, strength, endurance, and flexibility). Sustained low-intensity exercise such as weight lifting is good for burning fat. Long endurance exercises such as prolonged running also are good for burning fat but require proportionally more protein than other forms of exercise. Compared to other forms of exercise, fast-paced aerobic activities such as sprinting and basketball are fueled proportionally more by carbohydrates. By including a variety of exercise types in your regular schedule of physical activity, you can improve all aspects of your physical fitness, capacity, weight control, and overall health.

The short-term and immediate benefit of a fitness program is the ability to perform your duties more easily and with less stress on your body. Over time, your body composition will improve with an increase in lean body mass and a decrease in fat. As your body improves, so will your mental health and your mood. Research has shown that regular exercise leads to improved mental func-

tioning, reduced depression and anxiety, and greater resilience to the effects
of physical and psychological stress. Physically fit individuals also sleep better
(more soundly and with fewer interruptions), are more resistant to cold viruses
and other infectious agents, and are less likely to develop heart disease, diabetes,
and osteoporosis. Finally, recent evidence suggests that physical fitness may even
help protect the human body from certain types of cancer (especially colon and
breast cancers) and degenerative brain diseases such as Alzheimer's disease.

HARSH ENVIRONMENTS

Until wars are fought indoors, environmental challenges such as climate and
altitude will be potentially critical factors for military operations and warfighter
performance. Harsh environments are typically classified as hot-wet (jungle and
tropical areas), hot-dry (deserts), cold-wet (temperate latitudes with near freez-
ing temperatures and rain/snow), or cold-dry (northern latitudes and arctic areas). High-altitude environments (above 6,000 feet) are also considered harsh
because they are often cold and dry and pose unique challenges associated with
lack of oxygen.

Fortunately, the human body possesses many mechanisms that support its
adaptation to harsh environments. The process of adaptation occurs gradually
over the course of days or weeks.
Even so, harsh environments will
typically have a negative effect on
your ability to perform physical
and cognitive work. All of your
physical and mental abilities will
suffer to some extent as you experience high temperature and hu-

SYMPTOMS OF HYPOTHERMIA
✓ Uncontrollable shivering
✓ Difficulty with complex tasks
✓ Confusion
✓ Grogginess
✓ Muscle weakness
✓ Loss of coordination
✓ Slurred speech

midity, low temperature, or high altitude. In extreme cases—even with proper
clothing and adaptation—the human body will reach its physiological limit. At
this point, human beings are unable to work without risking physical injury or
possibly even death.

HEAT AND HUMIDITY

Physical adaptation to a very warm environment takes place over a period of five
to seven days after arrival in the hot climate. This process is activated by working and exercising for progressively longer periods of time at gradually greater

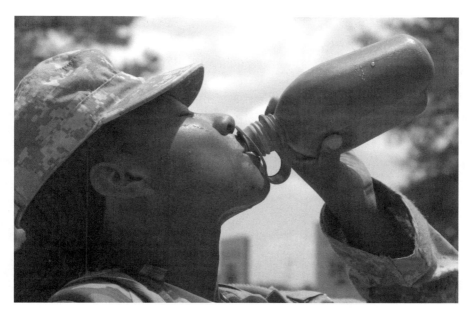

Pvt. Shantes Baxter takes a drink from her canteen during a break from basic combat training. *Photo courtesy of the U.S. Army/Crystal Lewis Brown, Fort Jackson Leader*

intensity. As your body begins to adapt, you will begin to sweat more and faster (you stay cooler), and your sweat will contain less salt (conserving essential electrolytes). Your blood circulation patterns will also change. Your blood will begin to flow more proportionally through your skin than through your body core. This allows your body to conduct work-generated heat to the skin, where it is dissipated. As you grow increasingly more accustomed to the hot climate, you will experience fewer dramatic increases in your heart rate when you are doing heavy work; this will allow you to work longer with less fatigue. Together, all of these adaptive changes improve your body's ability to rid itself of heat and accomplish work without succumbing to heat-related injury. It is more difficult to maintain a normal body temperature in hot-humid conditions. This is because heat loss through evaporative cooling is less efficient in high humidity. As a result, it is more difficult to work in the jungle than in a dry desert environment.

Hot weather affects all physical and cognitive abilities, even in physically fit individuals whose bodies have acclimated to the heat. This is generally true in temperatures above 85°F when relative humidity is above 75 percent. Simple reaction-time tasks (e.g., the speed of detecting a target) may be largely unaffected by heat and humidity, but any task that involves more complex or difficult choices (e.g., identifying the difference between friend and foe) may require several extra critical seconds to be performed accurately in hot, humid conditions. Heat will also affect your performance on tasks that require dexterity, steadiness, or aiming. In hot weather, you may be less able to assemble equipment, manipulate mechanical devices such as joystick controls, and fire individual or crew-served weapons.

Tasks that require sustained attention for hours at a time (e.g., sentry duty, instrument monitoring, and vehicle operations) are most affected by the heat. Your performance on these tasks can degrade significantly after just thirty minutes of continuous duty in a hot environment. You may also find it more difficult to perform quickly and accurately on tasks that involve memory, spatial reasoning (map reading), mathematical reasoning, or operational awareness (updating situation maps).

Heat and humidity cause personal discomfort and may even cause visual distortion or the imagined perception of visual images (mirages). Subjective experiences and personal discomfort can make many tasks and interactions even more difficult. For example, hot weather can interfere with effective communication because people tend to feel on edge in hot weather. Don't be surprised if social interactions are also more difficult as a result.

COLD AND HIGH ALTITUDE

The human body does not adapt as readily to cold as it does to heat. This is probably due in some part to our tropical evolutionary history and the fact that we can limit exposure to the cold by adding protective layers of clothing. Even so, the human body does show some changes in response to cold. For example, after prolonged exposure (several weeks) in a cold environment, your body will not begin to shiver until it has cooled to a lower core temperature. This is a useful adaptation because although shivering generates bodily warmth, shivering also causes the body to lose its heat more rapidly.

> **SYMPTOMS OF FROSTBITE**
>
> ✓ Upon exposure to cold, skin becomes numb and turns to a gray or waxy-white color.
> ✓ Initial sensation is tingling, burning, aching, and cold/sharp pain.
> ✓ Finally, there is numbness.

Another physical response to cold is that the blood vessels in your hands and feet will open (dilate) to flood these areas with warm blood and thus prevent or delay cold-related injury such as frostbite. After prolonged exposure to

Airmen and soldiers deliver humanitarian aid to snowbound villages in the Parwan District of Afghanistan. *U.S. Air Force photo by Capt. Catie Hague*

a cold environment, this response begins to occur more rapidly than it would otherwise.

A person cooled by exposure to a cold environment cannot perform efficiently. Cold affects your ability to perform tasks that require fine motor skills and manual dexterity, such as handling and working with small weapons pieces. Your ability to feel things with your fingers is diminished by cold. Studies have shown that as your core temperature is reduced (hypothermia), the blood flow in your brain and the speed at which your nerve fibers conduct important impulses actually slows down. This interferes with your ability to complete complex cognitive tasks (such as vigilance and computerized tracking tasks) and slows your response to auditory and visual signals. When your body temperature cools, you are more likely to make errors of judgment and have memory problems. First, your speech may slur, making it difficult if not impossible to communicate effectively with others. If your body cools to approximately 86° F, you will be unable to function and will likely fall unconscious. Hypothermia occurs more quickly in water or under wet conditions. Your body cools faster when it is wet. Those who work in or under water should be aware that safe operating times are much shorter as a result.

Human cognitive abilities can be significantly affected when the body reaches altitudes above approximately 9,000 feet above sea level. However, lower pressure makes it more difficult for the body to capture oxygen and thus work or exercise even at much lower altitudes. Your physical abilities can be significantly affected at altitudes starting as low as 6,000 feet above sea level, which is ground-level altitude in Colorado Springs, Colorado. Just north of Colorado Springs is the U.S. Air Force Academy, at an altitude of 7,258 feet above sea level. At this altitude, visiting athletic teams may find it very difficult to compete with acclimated Air Force cadets.

Although muscle strength and brief muscular contraction power are generally unaffected by altitude, most people lose at least some weight at high altitude, and this can lead to a loss of muscle mass. Weight loss at high altitude may be due to a change in the body's preference for carbohydrates or to a general decrease in appreciation for the taste of food. If you are working at high altitude, it is important to maintain your usual food intake so as to preserve muscle mass and maintain your ability to work as best you can under the circumstances.

When you first ascend to a high altitude, you will experience a profound initial decrease in your ability to perform vigorous work or sustain even low-intensity physical activity without rest. The effect is especially pronounced for aerobic activities such as running or cycling, which require sustained physical effort. Generally speaking, the human body expends a greater percentage of its maximal aerobic capacity at elevations at least 6,000 feet above sea level. The difference becomes steadily more dramatic at higher altitudes and can have a significant effect on your ability to perform straightforward but critical physical tasks such as carrying items or moving heavy objects.

To compensate for the reduced availability of oxygen at high altitude, your heart must beat faster to pump more blood to your muscles. You must also breathe faster. As you acclimate to the higher altitude over the course of several weeks or months, your heart rate and blood flow will return to normal levels, where they would be at sea level. As your body acclimates to high altitude, it begins to produce more red blood cells, which allows your blood to deliver more oxygen with less effort from your heart. However, your breathing rate will probably remain somewhat faster than at sea level. Depending on the altitude, you may simply never acclimate fully to be able to perform all physical tasks as well as you could at sea level.

Your senses will also be affected at high altitudes due to lower oxygen availability. Vision is affected first, even at altitudes as low as 5,000 feet above sea level. At 9,000 feet, you will experience changes in night vision, dark adaptation, visual acuity, and color discrimination. Although your ability to hear pure tones will not be affected, research has shown that you will be slower to process the sounds (e.g., consonants) that are associated with speech. This can have a direct impact on your ability to understand sentences that are spoken through radio transmissions.

High altitude affects all cognitive abilities, including those necessary for psychomotor, memory, and reaction-time tasks. Rifle marksmanship is significantly impaired for up to three days, and reaction times (e.g., target detection) are slower. At high altitude, you may also experience mood changes that persist for several days. Warfighters working at high altitudes report feeling irritable, less friendly, anxious, and sometimes confused due to difficulties associated with clear thinking. The higher the altitude, the more severe these effects can be. In one research study, even a relatively small increase in altitude from 13,800 to 15,500 feet was associated with significant changes in mood as well as decreased cognitive performance. At very high altitudes (18,000 feet and above), all abilities—physical and cognitive—are impaired, and the human body simply cannot adapt to compensate. In addition to the worsening of physical performance, cognitive abilities, and mood changes, these changes will also take longer to recover from exposure to increasingly higher altitudes.

PREPARATION AND PROTECTION

You can protect yourself from all harsh environments by having and using appropriate clothing and equipment, training, and your knowledge of adaptation. You can facilitate adaptation by taking good care of yourself prior to deployment. When living and working in harsh environments, it is crucial to be healthy

Low-altitude air defense gunners climb a hill for a good position to engage notional aviation targets during training at landing zone Falcon at Marine Corps Mountain Warfare Training Center, Bridgeport, California. *U.S. Marine Corps/Cpl. Nicole A. LaVine*

and physically fit. Maintain adequate food and water intake and do your best to get enough sleep on as normal a cycle as possible. Train and overtrain to ensure your skills are as sharp as possible. This will help to lessen the impact of any temporary performance changes that may be linked to harsh environmental conditions. Remember that when you are working in a harsh environment, you should allow additional time to ensure accuracy.

Adaptation to any harsh environment takes time. Adaptation to a hot climate requires that you make safe, gradual increases in the intensity and time of your work over a period of approximately one week. You must also be aware that thirst alone is not an adequate indicator of dehydration; instead, monitor the color of your urine, which should be the color of weak lemonade. If you are working in very cold conditions, be sure that you are wearing all available protective clothing and seek help if you experience symptoms of frostbite or hypothermia.

> **IMPORTANT!**
>
> Make sure to drink enough water when you are acclimating to a hot climate. Adequate hydration will greatly improve your ability to adapt and work in hot weather.

If you are ascending to a high altitude, it is recommended that you go through a process of "staging," which should involve limited incremental ascents and layover periods of several days. The recommended layover period is one day of residence at the new altitude for every 1,000 feet of subsequent elevation you plan to ascend. This approach will greatly reduce your risk of developing altitude-related illnesses such as acute mountain sickness (nausea, headache, malaise) or more serious and potentially life-threatening changes such as pulmonary or cerebral edema (buildup of fluid in the lungs or brain).

Finally, it is very important to be psychologically prepared with a positive outlook and good expectations. Put faith in your clothing and equipment. Have confidence in your abilities. Be reminded that you are working within a cohesive unit and you have been trained to handle the challenge. Know that virtually no matter where you go on earth, other human beings have gone before and in many cases have lived there for thousands of years. You can adapt to live and work there, too.

SLEEP AND SLEEP DEPRIVATION

In the opening days of the Gulf War, operational tempo (OPTEMPO) was high. Crews from the 2nd Armored Cavalry Regiment had gotten very little sleep. An armored platoon of Bradley fighting vehicles set up a screen line to monitor for Iraqi units. As night fell, they relied upon thermal sights to identify a column of approaching vehicles as Iraqi armored personnel carriers. A brief fight took place in which all the Iraqi vehicles were destroyed. After the battle, it was found that two of our own Bradley fighting vehicles had also been hit—by friendly fire. Fortunately, the crews of the damaged Bradleys escaped without injury.

(Based on a February 1991 incident report)

Two factors contributed to the incident described above. First, the battle took place during the early morning hours, when mental performance is at its worst. Second, the American troops were chronically sleep deprived. Because of these factors, some of the troops became spatially disoriented. They lost their ability to adjust quickly to a changing situation, and they mistook what was in front of them. Interestingly, their high-level cognitive functions (adaptive reasoning, orientation) were impaired, but their ability to swiftly and accurately put the crosshairs on the target during the short battle remained intact.

There is no doubt about it—lack of sleep is bad for the brain. When we don't get enough sleep, our mental abilities suffer. The abilities that require the most intense cognitive processing are most affected, while overtrained mental and psychomotor skills are least affected. Sleep deprivation can have serious consequences for soldiers in training and in the field. Here, we will consider why sleep is needed, how much is needed, and what can be done when the demands of your mission prevent you from getting an adequate amount of sleep.

WHY MUST WE SLEEP?

Many theories exist about why the human body needs sleep. The theory that has gained the most support from scientific research suggests that sleep is necessary to restore energy. The brain needs energy to function, and it gets this energy from glucose (a simple carbohydrate/sugar found in food). Glucose is used to make energy molecules (adenosine triphosphate), which are stored in the brain's cells until needed. Brain cells are fueled by ATP, which when broken down releases energy and other products, including adenosine. The longer you are awake, the more adenosine builds up inside your brain cells. Some adenosine must then be transported out of the cells. In specific parts of the brain, this extracellular adenosine acts on other sleep regulatory cells to make you sleepy.

When you sleep, extracellular adenosine then returns into your brain cells for conversion into ATP energy molecules, which are used again to make energy. As extracellular levels of adenosine decrease, so does your need for sleep. The result is that by sleeping, you restore the energy that your brain needs to function.

SLEEP, LEARNING, AND PERFORMANCE

The biological need for sleep to maintain brain energy levels probably explains why sleep is necessary to maintain cognitive abilities. Sleep is also important to enable learning of new tasks, mental as well as physical. If you are entirely

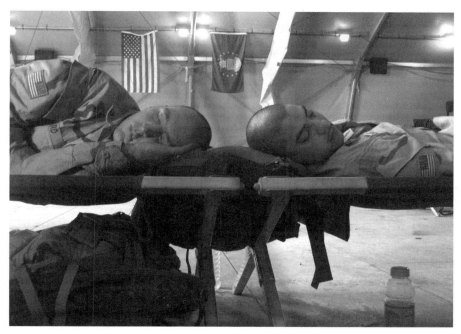

Soldiers catch up on sleep at Manas Air Base in Kyrgyzstan. *U.S. Air Force photo by Staff Sgt. J Russell Martin*

Marines take a nap after landing on the beach near Camp Lemonier, Djibouti. *U.S. Marine Corps/Petty Officer 2nd Class Jesse B. Awalt*

deprived of sleep for twenty-four to forty-eight hours, or if you get less than normal daily amounts of sleep for several days or weeks, you may suffer serious effects on your ability to think accurately and quickly, analyze new situations, and process or integrate new information.

Studies by military researchers have shown that for some tasks, your efficiency will be reduced by as much as 25 percent for every twenty-four hours of sleep you have been deprived. When your sleep is restricted to just a few (three to four) hours each night, you will quickly begin to suffer significant deficits in your performance on tasks that require speed and accuracy (e.g., vigilance and reaction time tasks). Studies have shown that people will make eleven times as many errors on cognitive tasks if they lose just two hours of sleep at night. After seven days of restricted sleep, your mental performance will be reduced to just a fraction (35–50 percent) of your usual abilities when you are fully rested. This is due not to the fact that you are more likely to fall asleep (which you are), but rather to the fact that when you have been deprived of sleep, your brain's ability to process information actually slows down. In critical situations at critical times,

An F-117A Nighthawk pilot takes an aviation simulation test as part of a research study on aviator fatigue. *Photo courtesy of the U.S. Air Force*

your slower response time could mean the difference between life and death.

If you have been deprived of sleep, you may experience micro-sleep, which is the loss of attention and failure to perceive and respond to external information. Micro-sleep can occur when you are fatigued or drowsy while trying to perform a monotonous task such as driving or staring at a television or computer. You might experience micro-sleep with your eyes open (blank stare) or eyes closed. Afterwards, you may have no memory of it. Micro-sleep episodes are usually brief, lasting a few seconds or a few minutes. However, even a brief period of micro-sleep can be dangerous in some situations. According to the U.S. National Highway Traffic

SLEEP FACTS
The brain needs sleep to function; the body needs simple rest.
For every 24 hours you stay awake, you can lose as much as 25% of your efficiency on cognitive tasks.
Complex cognitive tasks such as map reading, plotting coordinates, and updating situational awareness are affected first and most by sleep deprivation.
When you lose just one night of sleep, your reasoning and complex task reaction time can be impaired as much as if you were legally drunk (blood alcohol level of 0.10%).
Chronic sleep restriction can have the same effects as complete sleep deprivation.
Short naps can have beneficial effects that last for hours.
Vaccines are more effective when you are fully rested.
You will learn new information and skills faster and better if you sleep after a practice training session before doing the task again.
Snoring may be a sign of a sleep disorder. If you snore chronically, ask your health care provider for more information.

Safety Administration, 40,000 injuries and 1,550 deaths occur every year because of drowsy drivers.

An adequate amount of sleep is also critical to your ability to learn new information and become proficient at new tasks. It is important to get enough sleep not just while you are learning new things but also during the period after initial learning, when you are practicing to improve your skills and performance.

After you practice a new task, a period of normal, restful sleep can improve your performance beyond the simple effects of practice itself. If you follow new learning with a period of restful sleep, your ability to learn new and complex mental problems will be improved, often with the benefit of greater insight. Researchers believe that sleep is necessary for the growth and consolidation of new brain pathways that form when we learn new mental and physical tasks. This is especially important in areas of the brain that control memory.

CIRCADIAN RHYTHM

Your body and brain processes undergo normal fluctuations throughout the twenty-four-hour period of a day. This daily cycle is referred to as your circadian rhythm. For example, your body temperature follows a strong circadian cycle. Your internal body temperature is normally at its lowest level in the early morning hours (between 0300 and 0500) and rises gradually to its highest level in the evening hours (around 2000). Scientific studies of cognitive performance have shown that our ability to perform mental tasks follows a similar circadian pattern. When faced with tasks that require cognitive abilities such as memory, attention, and information analysis, we perform most poorly during the early morning and best during the early evening. Some studies indicate that fluctuations in mental performance lag one to two hours behind fluctuations in internal body temperature. It is helpful to be aware of these daily fluctuations and consider their potential impact upon your physical and cognitive performance at different times of the day.

As we discussed earlier, sleepiness is governed in large part by the length of time you have been awake and your brain's need to metabolize and renew its energy level. Sleepiness is also governed by the natural circadian rhythm, which is synchronized to the cycle of daylight and darkness that occurs wherever you normally live.

Even if you are fully rested and have traveled to an entirely different time zone, you will naturally begin to feel sleepy during the hours that would normally define pre-dawn or early morning wherever you have been living. This is the basis for what we know more commonly as jet lag. The clock in the Middle East may tell you it is noon, but your body may still believe the time of day is 0400. As a result, you are sleepy and less mentally sharp. You may also have trouble going to sleep at night because your body believes it is still much earlier in the day and your mind is full of energy. Your sleep cycles and other physical and mental processes will gradually adjust and eventually synchronize to new environments and time zones. Although this process is slower for older individuals (mid-forties and above) than for younger people, as a general rule of thumb, you can expect that you will need approximately one full day to adjust to each hour of difference in the new time zone. You should also be aware that it is generally more difficult to adjust when you are traveling eastward (advancing/losing time) than when traveling westward (gaining time).

How Much Sleep Is Enough, and How Can You Get It?

In general, it is ideal for the human body to get eight hours of sleep every twenty-four hours. Most people get their daily sleep during one extended period of time, usually at night. However, it can also be extremely effective to sleep for shorter periods of time at various times throughout the day. This sleep discipline strategy can help to prevent the effects of sleep deprivation in military settings where it is impossible to sleep for more extended periods of time.

Sleep discipline refers to the practice of getting as much sleep as you can on a regular basis and sleeping whenever you can to make up for restricted or disrupted sleep. Good sleep discipline is as important as adequate hydration. You will help no one by failing to get an adequate amount of sleep.

Napping is one effective means to compensate for lost sleep. Strictly speaking, a nap is defined as any period of sleep that is less than half as long as your ordinary sleep period. More generally, we think of a nap as a period of sleep lasting between thirty minutes and an hour or two. Naps don't just feel good—they actually restore mental function and alertness. When sleep has been restricted to fewer than five hours per night, a simple thirty-minute nap during the day can significantly improve alertness for a period of two to six hours after the nap. Even shorter periods of sleep (ten to fifteen minute "power naps") are beneficial to immediately restore and invigorate the body and to improve mental performance significantly.

Some people avoid naps because they dislike the groggy feeling they experience immediately after waking up. This experience is known more formally as sleep inertia, and it is especially common

SLEEP HYGIENE

Sleep hygiene refers to practices associated with encouraging effective sleep. You can improve your ability to sleep by paying attention to how and where you do it.

- ✓ Try to sleep in a comfortable, cool, and darkened location if possible. Remember that your body is sensitive to light. If necessary, cover windows with light-blocking shades or wear a sleep mask.
- ✓ Move away from noise and commotion if possible. Try to find a sleeping location that is removed from the noise of operations, daytime activities, and areas of heavy vehicle or foot traffic. Use foam earplugs to reduce ambient noise.
- ✓ Limit your use of caffeine. Avoid caffeine entirely during the evening hours.
- ✓ Avoid smoking before you try to sleep. (Nicotine is a stimulant.)
- ✓ Alcohol may make you feel sleepy, but it will also disrupt your normal sleep cycles. If you consume alcohol, you will feel less well rested when you wake up.
- ✓ Avoid eating a big meal or protein-rich snacks before you try to sleep. Light snacks that contain carbohydrates may be more helpful.
- ✓ Do not participate in vigorous exercise within 3 hours of trying to sleep. Note, however, that individuals who regularly maintain their aerobic fitness also tend to sleep more soundly than those who do not.

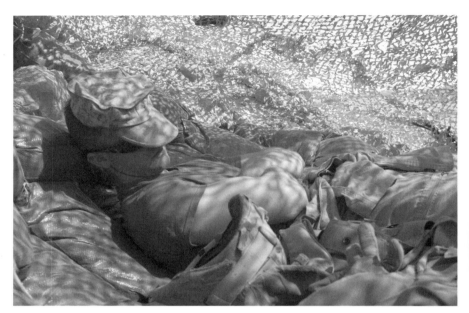

U.S. Marine catches a nap between shifts of perimeter security during a bridge reconstruction mission in the Al Anbar Province of Iraq. *U.S. Marine Corps/Lance Cpl. Brandon L. Roach*

after naps taken in the early morning. You should understand that sleep inertia is usually brief. The restorative benefits of a good nap far outweigh whatever temporary difficulty you may experience in waking up. If you are able to take a nap prior to a military operation, it will facilitate improved performance by helping to reduce or prevent the negative impact of prolonged periods of wakefulness. Just as runners perform better when they drink water before a race (versus simply trying to replace it during the race), you will perform better when you begin your work fully rested.

Managing Sleep Deprivation

If the demands of a military mission make it impossible for you to get enough sleep, there are actions you can take to improve your situation, your performance, and your ultimate survivability. First, pay careful attention to your equipment and how it works. Make changes if necessary. Redesign, modify, and retrofit as best you can to reduce the likelihood of errors and to conserve your energy by making your equipment as easy as possible to use. Develop routines that you can perform as accurately and automatically as possible. Train and overtrain until you can perform critical tasks with as little effort as possible. Work with your unit to develop and adhere to appropriate work-rest cycles. This should include rotating crews to support long operations.

Studies conducted at the National Training Center have shown that staff soldiers whose tasks require the greatest amount of cognitive input are also those who are least likely to get adequate amounts of sleep. Effective performance on a complex and dynamic battlefield requires clear and adaptable thinking from military planners, leaders, and operators.

Leaders should develop efficient leadership tactics to reduce unnecessary demands on their subordinates. Leaders should also do their best to exemplify and enforce sleep discipline and sleep hygiene techniques as described above.

If you are being sent on a long-distance deployment, one very helpful preparation strategy is to get on destination time prior to departure. This can be done gradually by going to bed and getting up at progressively earlier times over the course of several days before deployment. Family situations and hectic preparations schedules may make this difficult to do, but it may be somewhat easier to achieve if the strategy is instituted on a unit basis. By gradually adapting in advance, you will find it easier to synchronize your sleep cycle to the new environment and different time zone when you arrive at your new destination. If you will be traveling eastward, it can also be helpful to take melatonin, which encourages sleep and will help you to reset your body's clock by falling asleep earlier in the evening. Continue taking melatonin for up to a week after you arrive at your destination. Studies of eastward travelers who work night duty hours suggest that a seven-day, low-dose regimen of melatonin (5–10 milligrams in the late afternoon or early evening) results in earlier sleep onset and longer sleep. For westbound travelers, melatonin administered during the second half of the night (e.g., by time-release formula taken before bedtime) improves sleep maintenance through the night.

It is understandable that you might have difficulty sleeping in a war zone. If earplugs and sleep masks don't help, consider trying melatonin (2–5 milligrams), which, in addition to helping reset your body clock, increases sleepiness, improves sleep quality, and helps next-day alertness. However, some research indicates that melatonin taken in doses greater than 1 milligram may impair post-sleep performance. This may be a problem in military settings where you could be called upon to wake quickly and resume operations. It is not known how much time may be required to achieve full alertness after higher doses of melatonin.

If you experience continued difficulty sleeping, you may be suffering from temporary insomnia. Consult with a physician or physician's assistant about possible use of prescription sleep aids. Over-the-counter medications may make you drowsy but generally do not improve the amount or quality of sleep. Take care to read label information. Over-the-counter sleep aids often contain an antihistamine that can have lingering effects after short periods of sleep. If you have trouble sleeping for an extended period of time, you should see a physician to rule out other underlying problems such as depression, pain, interrupted breathing, or neurological disease.

Most people are familiar with the effects of caffeine, which can temporarily compensate for lack of sleep by improving alertness and performance. Caffeine can be found in cola, coffee, and in many energy drinks. How much caffeine you ingest will vary by the size of the drink.

HOW DOES CAFFEINE WORK?

Caffeine is a temporary solution to sleepiness.

Caffeine stimulates wakefulness by blocking certain receptors on cells in the brain. When these receptors are blocked, extracellular adenosine cannot bind to them. Without the effect of adenosine, you don't feel sleepy.

Caffeine does not reduce your need for sleep. Caffeine does not restore your brain's energy level.

CAFFEINE AND NAPS

An intelligent schedule of naps and caffeine may be your most effective strategy for managing sleep deprivation.

For example:

If you are about to embark on an extended operation or face a prolonged period of sleep deprivation, take a 4-hour nap during the day, followed by caffeine (200 mg) during the night.

After an extended period of operations or wakefulness, take caffeine immediately before wakefulness, take caffeine immediately before a 30–60 minute nap. This will allow you to fall asleep before the caffeine takes effect. You will wake up sooner, feeling more refreshed.

Even the relatively small amount of caffeine (approximately 50 mg) found in the typical 12-ounce can of cola can help to improve performance on vigilance and reaction time tasks. Larger amounts (200 mg = typical large cup of coffee) can prevent performance degradation on vigilance tasks such as those performed during three hours of sentry duty. These higher doses of caffeine do not affect marksmanship ability and can be effective during prolonged periods of total sleep deprivation. However, it is important to note that you should not exceed 600 mg in a single ingestion.

If you need to use caffeine, the best strategy is to take an initial dose of 100–200 mg just as you begin to feel mental fatigue is setting in. Then space subsequent additional 100 mg doses approximately three to four hours apart. Caffeine can be taken directly in the form of over-the-counter tablets (usually 100–200 mg). Some tablets are produced as sustained-release formulations, which provide an immediate initial boost followed by a prolonged lasting effect. Note that sustained-release caffeine pills may make it difficult to sleep if an unexpected opportunity arises. Another alternative is caffeine gum (100 mg per stick), the effects of which are less sustained but felt more quickly. It is not recommended that you chew more than three sticks of caffeine gum during a three-hour period.

STRESS: THE MIND-BODY CONNECTION

A growing body of medical and psychological evidence tells us that there is a very real and predictable effect of stress (physical or psychological) on your body's ability to resist illness. Your immune system is a marvelous and complex system whose purpose is to identify and neutralize organisms that might otherwise cause disease. Chronic stress can increase your vulnerability to illness. This risk is especially great when you endure high work demands over which you have little or no control, or when you are dealing with sustained personal or family problems that are difficult to resolve. These stresses do not make you sick directly. Rather, they weaken your immune system and thus make it more difficult to resist illness.

Scientific studies have shown that individuals who are under high levels of stress get more colds and heal more slowly from cuts and bruises. Studies of soldiers undergoing intense training (e.g., Ranger training) that involves sleep deprivation and prolonged hunger show that their immune systems are compromised by these conditions. As a result, they are more vulnerable to infections such as cellulitis.

Different factors contribute to how you cope with stress and how dramatically it affects your body. Some factors are related to personality characteristics, life experiences, diet, exercise, and family or social circumstances. Some factors are probably related to your genetic history. The best way to counter stress is to prepare for it in advance by optimizing your personal and social behavior in ways that can protect you against the most harmful effects of stress.

Maintain strong family ties and build a reliable network of friends and neighbors. Research has shown that individuals who have strong social networks also have better functioning immune systems. These individuals are better equipped to fight acute and chronic disease.

Leaders should conduct activities and adopt a leadership style that promotes unit cohesion and strong morale.

Become as proficient as possible in the skills required by your job. You will handle stress better if you feel confident in your ability to perform your duties.

View stressful situations as challenges to be met and overcome rather than as overwhelming obstacles or threats. Talk to others about how you can solve problems creatively, as a team.

Focus on your work ethic and your commitment to your family, your unit, and your country. These motivators will remind you of the meaning of your work, which in turn will help you to keep stress in perspective.

Do your best to be optimistic. Try to have a positive attitude and share it with others.

Seek help as quickly as possible from mental health professionals if you feel depressed or have traumatic memories. Early support can mean the difference between temporary difficulty and lasting symptoms of exposure to stress. This same guidance applies to family and financial struggles. Ask for help.

GOOD ADVICE FOR HEALTH AND SAFETY

Exercise regularly. Exercise makes and keeps you physically fit, healthy, and better able to withstand physical and mental stress.

Watch your weight. Weight control promotes health and good performance. Weight problems are usually due to overeating and lack of exercise.

Stop using nicotine. You will notice an immediate improvement in aerobic capacity, and you will dramatically reduce your risk of cancer, emphysema, stroke, and heart disease.

Get enough sleep. Set and keep regular sleep patterns as much as possible, even on weekends.

Protect your body. Use your protective gear as recommended (goggles, sunglasses, ear plugs, insect repellent, protective clothing, etc.). Practice safe, protected sex to avoid sexually transmitted diseases and prevent unintended pregnancy.

Prevent illness. Practice good field hygiene and sanitation. Keep your vaccines up to date.

Avoid misuse and abuse of alcohol. Alcohol does not promote good physical health. Heavy drinking is especially dangerous. Do you or does someone you know have a drinking problem? Familiarize yourself with criteria for abuse and dependence. If you are drinking to cope with stress or trauma, you may be at risk.

CHAPTER THREE

Understanding and Dealing with Stress

Elite athletes in all sports develop routines to help them perform well in competition. No athlete wants to choke or freeze under pressure. To avoid these reactions, athletes practice their skills. Practice builds confidence as it allows trained skills to become more automatic and supports more effective decision-making under pressure.

What works well for athletes can also work for military personnel. As a soldier, you need to be on top of your game whether you are stationed in garrison, active in field exercises, or engaged in combat. This is why training, rehearsal, and realistic field experience are so important. When you practice donning chemical protective clothing, your goal is to develop your skill so that you can suit up quickly and successfully without fear or clumsiness. When you practice clearing a weapons stoppage, your goal is to learn to perform this task virtually without thinking about it so that no precious seconds are lost in the heat of battle.

The first thing to understand about stress is that stress itself is not an inherently bad thing. Although we usually think of stress in negative terms, in many cases, stress can lead to good things. The results of a stressful situation will depend heavily upon how you respond to it. As you read this chapter, consider how you have responded to stress at other times in your life. In many cases, you probably responded in ways that led to a positive outcome. In an emergency, you may have experienced a surge of stress-related energy that literally saved your life. You may have received an unexpectedly high grade on a test in school. Meanwhile, in the absence of any stress whatsoever, you may have experienced times when you felt bored and unmotivated. As human beings, we actually thrive on a certain amount of stress. When we embrace stress as a challenge—not as a threat—it can motivate us to work harder and meet new goals. In return, we enjoy a unique sense of accomplishment. The more difficult it is to do something, the better we feel when we overcome the difficulty and achieve the task.

Research indicates that military service is among the most stressful of all professions or occupations. During the course of your military career, you will be exposed to a wide variety of stresses, including some of the most extreme challenges that human beings can encounter. Just as troops on patrol need armor to protect their bodies, soldiers also need "Kevlar for the mind" (resilience) to protect them from negative or extreme effects of stress. You can enhance your resilience to stress by learning more about how stress can affect the human body and brain.

When you perceive a threatening event or circumstance that is beyond your control, you experience stress. Your response to this situation may or may not be similar to that of the person standing next to you. One individual may experience a sudden headache or the sensation of butterflies in his stomach, while another begins to sweat or tremble. Although the symptoms and extent of each individual's stress response may be different, the basic physical processes that

Soldiers breach a house to search for insurgent activities during an operation in Zaghiniyat, Iraq. *Photo courtesy of the U.S. Army/Staff Sgt. Joann Makinano*

TABLE 3.1
THE AUTONOMIC NERVOUS SYSTEM

"Fight or Flight"	"Rest and Digest"
Sympathetic Nervous System (SNS)	*Parasympathetic Nervous System (PNS)*
Dilates pupils	Contracts pupils
Relaxes bronchi	Constricts bronchi
Speeds heart rate	Slows heart rate
Inhibits digestion	Stimulates digestion
Contracts vessels	Dilates vessels

initiate the stress response are similar. To understand the human body's response to stress, we must consider biology, psychology, and environment.

"FIGHT OR FLIGHT"

In 1914, physiologist Walter Cannon coined the term "fight or flight" to describe the essential aspects of the stress response. Through his research, Cannon had observed that when faced with danger, animals can respond in one of two ways. They can hold their ground and face the threat directly (fight) or they can avoid danger by fleeing from it (flight). When the fight-or-flight response is triggered by perceived threat or danger, the autonomic nervous system (ANS) is activated. The ANS controls the activity of many organs such as the heart, stomach, and intestines. Most of the time, we are unaware of these activities because they are involuntary and reflexive.

The ANS includes two subsystems, known separately as the sympathetic nervous system (SNS) and the parasympathetic nervous system (PNS). As a general rule, it is the job of the SNS to mobilize the body for action. The PNS, by contrast, directs the body toward rest and recuperation. Most of the time, the SNS and PNS maintain a functional balance (homeostasis). However, when the fight-or-flight response is triggered by stress, the SNS takes charge and stimulates action through the release of neurochemicals (e.g., adrenalin) and hormones (e.g., cortisol). These substances exert a dramatic effect on critical systems throughout the body. They stimulate an increase in heart rate and breathing. They also constrict blood vessels in many parts of the body. In the face of a deadly threat, these effects can be so intense that an individual may suffer stress-related diarrhea.

It is not uncommon for a person under life-threatening stress to lose bladder and bowel control as his body literally unloads its waste.[1] The SNS response redirects the body's energy to brain, lungs, and heart. As these organs receive increased blood supply, they will be better prepared for whatever action is necessary to ensure survival.

In the decades following Cannon's original observations, endocrinologist Hans Selye dramatically expanded our knowledge of how the human body adapts to stress from its initial alarm (SNS) response through its efforts to resist and cope with stress and, perhaps finally, to its eventual exhaustion from unrelenting stress. Selye's observations were so important that he is sometimes referred to as the "father of stress" and has been credited for having sparked the development of stress research as a unique field of biological study.

Another researcher, psychologist Richard Lazarus, changed our understanding of how thoughts and emotions can influence one's ability to cope with stress. Lazarus's research demonstrated that how we react to stress can depend upon (1) how we appraise the stressful situation, and (2) what we believe about our own ability to cope with it. In other words, our minds play a critical role in how we react to stress emotionally and physiologically. The objective reality of stress can be far less important than our perception of it and our confidence in confronting it. For example, how intensely the SNS reacts depends not upon how threatening the situation actually is but rather on how threatening you perceive the situation to be. If you are confronted with an unanticipated deadly threat and have little time to react, your SNS response can be extreme.

A common myth is that people who confront extreme stress will rise to the challenge and exhibit extraordinary strength, skills, or problem-solving abilities.

SIGNS AND SYMPTOMS OF STRESS

Physical Symptoms
- ✓ Changes in breathing pattern
- ✓ Muscle tension
- ✓ Headaches
- ✓ Heart palpitations
- ✓ High blood pressure
- ✓ Increased heart rate
- ✓ Digestive problems
- ✓ Susceptibility to illness

Cognitive/Emotional Changes
- ✓ Feeling out of control
- ✓ Feelings of anxiety/depression
- ✓ Distractibility
- ✓ Decreased concentration
- ✓ Irrational thoughts
- ✓ Increased anger/irritability

Behavioral Signs
- ✓ Overeating
- ✓ Loss of appetite
- ✓ Increased caffeine/sugar use
- ✓ Increased alcohol/drug use
- ✓ Increased smoking
- ✓ Social withdrawal
- ✓ Decreased professional commitment

Members of the visit, board, search, and seizure team of the guided-missile cruiser USS Chosin (CG 65) practice boarding techniques. Chosin is the flagship of Combined Joint Task Force (CTF) 151, a multinational task force established to conduct counter-piracy operations off the coast of Somalia. *U.S. Navy photo by Mass Communication Specialist 2nd Class Daniel Edgington*

In truth, extreme stress often provokes irrational thoughts and behavior. Intense activation of the SNS can cause irrational thinking and loss of muscle control.

Individuals who confront sudden, extreme stress may experience tunnel vision, loss of depth perception, reduced hearing, and deterioration of fine motor skills. They may become less capable of performing difficult tasks. Military trainers understand this process. The point of military training is to subject trainees to realistically stressful scenarios in which they can experience and learn to adapt to their own intense SNS reactions. By exposure and rehearsal, fighters are better equipped to keep their heads when confronted with the realities of combat.

THE AMYGDALA: THE BRAIN'S ALARM CENTER

The term "amygdala" comes from the Greek word for almond and refers to an almond-shaped cluster of structures situated just above the human brain stem. Psychologist Daniel Goleman compares the amygdala to an "alarm company where operators stand ready to send out emergency calls to the fire department, police, and a neighbor whenever a home security systems signals trouble." When you detect or perceive a threat, the amygdala issues an alarm signal that activates other centers in the brain and body. The amygdala can move us to action even before we are able to fully comprehend the situation or plan a measured response. Simply put, the amygdala provokes us to act before we think. In certain situations (e.g., an ambush or IED attack), this immediate reaction can make the difference between life and death or serious injury. In other situations, such as dismounted operations in urban environments, the same impulsive reaction may be more dangerous than it is helpful. By its urgency and intensity, the amygdala's alarm response interferes with careful decision-making and may provoke fear or anger out of proportion to the actual threat.

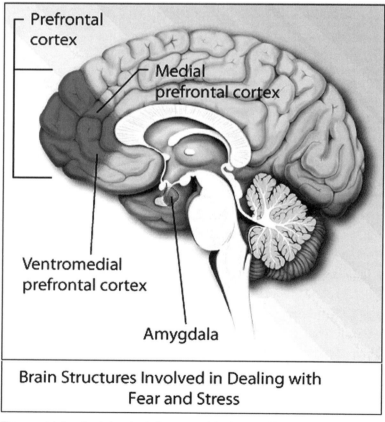

Prefrontal cortex

Medial prefrontal cortex

Ventromedial prefrontal cortex

Amygdala

Brain Structures Involved in Dealing with Fear and Stress

The amygdala is active in learning to fear an event (such as touching a hot stove) and in the early stages of learning not to fear. When the prefrontal cortex identifies stress as controllable, it suppresses the amygdala and controls the stress response. *National Institutes of Health*

A member of the Marine Attack Squadron 211 looks out at the lagoon in the center of the Wake Island atoll where a handful of Marines helped defend the island from an overwhelming Japanese invasion force before it was captured in 1941. *U.S. Marine Corps/Gunnery Sgt. Bill Lisbon*

Another important role of the amygdala is to stimulate emotional reactions and emotional memories. The amygdala serves as a storage area for vivid emotional memories, and it primes the body to react to such experiences. Experiences of events involving extreme emotions such as fear and exhilaration are among our strongest memories. Our brains store these experiences in a way that strengthens our ability to respond to similar situations in the future. While this is generally a protective process, the power of emotional memories can also interfere with recovery from exposure to trauma. Persistent and unwanted recall of traumatic experiences may be associated with fear, anxiety, and related physiological reactions. If these difficulties are left untreated and uncontrolled, posttraumatic stress disorder (PTSD) may be the result. Although it is not always possible to prevent PTSD, it can be resolved if treated properly.

TURNING OFF THE STRESS RESPONSE

The same processes that activate the stress response can also turn it off. The SNS and PNS have reciprocal effects, pulling the body's critical systems and processes in opposite directions to avoid dangerous extremes. The SNS activates chemical and hormonal changes that characterize the stress response, and the PNS acts to slow the stress response. You can engage the PNS voluntarily to reduce or turn off your stress response. Proven methods include controlled breathing, meditation, muscle relaxation, and cognitive coping techniques.

When a perceived threat is reduced or removed, the various hormones and chemicals released in response to stress are quickly metabolized in the bloodstream. It is important that your stress response be relieved and that your body returns to its pre-stress baseline status. If the original threat message to your brain is not turned off and your body stays in its fight-or-flight response condition for a long period of time, your physical and emotional health may suffer. Chronic stress can have many undesirable effects on health and well-being. Physicians and researchers have observed the negative effects of chronic stress to include suppressed immune response and slower healing from injuries and illness. Chronic stress is a risk factor for some serious illnesses such as coronary artery disease, peptic ulcers, diabetes, and cancer. Chronic stress can also affect your perception of life events and challenges. In the context of chronic stress, problems that once seemed manageable might suddenly seem urgent and overwhelming.

If you think you may be dealing with chronic stress, it is wise to consult with a mental health professional who can work with you on an individual basis to consider useful strategies for relief. Meanwhile, it may be very helpful to engage your body's own resources by practicing meditation, controlled breathing, or muscle relaxation. These simple techniques can engage your PNS to reduce the effects of ongoing stress. More will be said about these strategies later in this chapter.

HOW STRESS AFFECTS YOUR PERFORMANCE

How well do you cope with pressure? For some people, the idea of taking a test or speaking in public causes extreme anxiety. They might even lose sleep over it. For others, these same demands are anticipated less anxiously and more simply as cause for reasoned concern and preparation. Different people can respond very differently to stressful circumstances. These individual differences are often related to how we perceive the situation and how we feel physically when we confront it.

How we respond to stress can depend very much on how we perceive and think about our environment. For example, if you are pessimistic about your ability to pass a test, your negative expectations or fears will likely increase your level of anxiety. In this case, you may be right to feel more anxious.

Temperatures of 115 °F combined with 60-plus pounds of combat gear can take its toll. *U.S. Marine Corps/ Staff Sgt. Jim Goodwin*

When it comes to stress, thoughts and ideas can exert a very real and measurable impact on human physical and cognitive performance. Even if you would otherwise be fully capable of passing a test or running a two-mile race, negative expectations and anxiety can prevent you from achieving your potential. While it is true that a moderate amount of stress may be helpful to motivate adequate preparation, persistently negative expectations can lead to excessive physiological arousal, which in turn interferes with cardiovascular and aerobic capacity. When we are overaroused, we experience many of the symptoms of a full-blown stress response, including increased heart rate and respiration and decreased blood flow to the extremities. Sweating, cramping, fatigue, shaking, and nausea may also occur. All of these reactions are detrimental to physical performance and may have additional negative effects on self-confidence and motivation. Stress and anxiety also interfere with cognitive processes such as attention, concentration, and memory, all of which are critical to effective performance. Seemingly harmless thoughts and fears can become self-fulfilling prophecy by reducing your real performance potential.

Just Enough Stress

While it is true that too much stress (overarousal) interferes in predictable ways with physical and mental performance, it is also true that too little stress may be indirectly detrimental to performance. In the complete absence of stress, motivation suffers. Unmotivated individuals put less effort into their preparation and performance. If you are too relaxed or calm about the task at hand, it may take longer for you to prepare or warm up. If you feel no stress at all prior to an important test or challenge, this probably means you aren't taking it seriously enough. This too will have predictable negative effects on your performance.

How much stress is enough? When you experience a moderate amount of stress, you may feel keyed up or excited, but also confident and hopeful. You will probably perceive the situation as a manageable challenge. This is when you are physically and psychologically prepared to perform at your best. From an aerobic standpoint, your lungs and muscles prepare themselves for what is about to come. Your blood flow increases gradually as your major organs prepare to work harder. Your attention is focused on the task at hand, and you think carefully about how best to prepare for and manage the challenge. To reach and maintain this moderate level of arousal, you must be motivated to prepare by training, practice, conditioning, or study. Preparation builds confidence, which in turn prevents overarousal.

COMMON MILITARY STRESSORS

Stress is an unavoidable fact of life in the military. It begins in basic training, when the stress of unfamiliar expectations and extreme demands may at times seem overwhelming. Stress is a part of military life in garrison, where expectations grow as do the demands of training and field exercises.

Garrison life provides an ideal opportunity to develop and practice good habits toward effective stress management, including regular exercise, good nutrition, effective communication with family and friends, and other strategies (e.g., meditation) that can help to prevent the possible negative effects of chronic stress. Certainly, you are aware that you may one day have to encounter the more extreme stress of life in combat. By learning to manage stress early in your military career, you can give yourself the advantage of preparation.

Overseas and Operational Deployments

Whatever your occupational specialty or destination, deployment is a stressful experience. Even if you do not experience combat, you will likely be forced to contend with the difficulties associated with adjustment to unfamiliar surroundings, harsh environments, strenuous and sometimes unpredictable schedules,

A firefighter deployed from Beale Air Force Base finds a few precious moments to talk with his wife by telephone. *U.S. Air Force photo by Staff Sgt. Alex Koenig*

and the lack of creature comforts. For most service members, the first and most difficult challenge of deployment is that it requires separation from family and friends. It is not only that we miss our loved ones when we are away but that time spent with family and friends also helps relieve stress. It is important to acknowledge this problem and compensate for it as best you can. Whenever possible, maintain regular and effective communication with those at home. In addition, get involved in any social activities that are available to you on location. Allow yourself to build a local network of social support that can provide occasional, much-needed relief from stress.

As much as you may miss your family, at some point you will likely have to deal with the additional stress of managing problems at home from a distance. Difficulties may develop involving family finances, behavioral issues, school performance, transportation, illness, and perhaps mistrust or misunderstanding as too often results from the hasty or careless use of e-mail. The best thing you can do for yourself and your family is to prepare well for your deployment. Organize your financial matters in advance. Have the family car serviced and repaired as necessary. Discuss new roles and responsibilities. Make sure everyone in the

Marines relax by playing a game of baseball and having a cookout. The game was organized to provide separated squads an opportunity to socialize. *U.S. Marine Corps/Sgt. Eric C. Schwartz*

family knows how and where to get help and medical care. Communicate clearly and effectively regarding your concerns, fears, and expectations. Develop a communications plan, acknowledging your own limitations and those that others might encounter in your absence. Once again, the more you do to prepare yourself and your loved ones for stress, the better equipped you and they will be to manage it.

RESILIENCE TO STRESS

As a trained military professional, you already enjoy a high level of confidence in your ability to confront and overcome physical and psychological hardships. Through your early military training, you learned that you can perform your duties under extreme conditions and in situations that challenge your professional dedication, your physical strength, and your mental stamina. Through experience, you will discover that in order to perform well under stress, you must be flexible, creative, adaptive, realistic, determined, focused, and driven by purpose and perspective. Simply put, you must be resilient.

How you conduct yourself on a daily basis will affect your overall level of preparation and readiness. If you are physically and psychologically healthy, you

Staff Sgt. Travis Snook beams confidence before the M4 qualification event of the 2007 Department of the Army Noncommissioned Officer/ Soldier of the Year Competition. *Photo courtesy of the U.S. Army/T. Anthony Bell, Fort Lee Public Affairs Office*

will be better prepared to handle the challenges of military operations and cope with the stress. It is easier to deal with stress if you have a positive view of yourself, your life, your work, and its meaning. How you manage your thoughts and physical reactions to stress—reactions that may be brief or may last for weeks, months, or even years—can also have a profound effect on how you approach new challenges in the future.

Resilience can be seen as a set of personality traits or characteristics, an assortment of learned skills or behavior, or a combination of both personality traits and behavior. No one is entirely resilient to all types of stress at all times. You might be generally resilient to certain types of stress while being extremely vulnerable to others. Whether you think of resilience as something you have (such as a personality trait or disposition), as something you believe (such as faith or a positive outlook), or as something you do (such as a plan, a strategy, or a way of behaving), nowhere is the need for resilience more compelling than in military combat where, in practical terms, resilience means survival itself. If you want not only to survive but also thrive and lead, you must develop thoughts, habits, behavior, and strategies that maximize your resilience by improving your psychological capacity, your flexibility, your adaptability, and your endurance.

HOW RESILIENT PEOPLE THINK, FEEL, AND BEHAVE

Resilience is not immunity. Being resilient does not mean that you won't experience stress. Resilient people are challenged by stress, and they feel its effects on mind, body, and behavior. But because they have developed resilience, they know

Navy diver comes to the surface of the water in the Bala Murgahab River in Afghanistan. *U.S. Navy photo by Mass Communication Specialist 1st Class Matthew Bash*

how to apply specific characteristics, beliefs, and strategies not only to reduce the negative impact of stress but also to use it to their benefit to improve job performance and long-term well-being.

Researchers have identified a fairly consistent set of characteristics and types of behavior that are typical of people who function effectively under stress. In general, resilient people:

- View themselves positively and have confidence in their abilities
- Are competent in work or activities that are valued by others
- Possess a sense of independence, autonomy, and control
- Are realistic in how they view themselves, other people, and situations
- Have supportive and trusting relationships with friends and/or family members
- Communicate well with others
- Possess beliefs and/or a sense of higher purpose that enable them to make meaning of positive as well as negative events in their lives
- Set manageable goals and take determined steps to reach those goals
- Are oriented toward problem solving
- Seek help when needed

- Have a strong sense of responsibility and control
- Maintain a sense of perspective and a positive or hopeful outlook
- Accept or embrace change as a part of life
- Participate in regular physical activities or exercise
- Confront difficulties by taking decisive initiative, acting with determination
- Can be flexible and creative in their thinking
- Are willing to try new strategies
- Have a sense of humor about themselves and about life
- Recall and consider previous challenges or stressful experiences in a productive way to identify or reinforce coping and/or problem solving

Some of these psychological and behavioral strategies may seem to come naturally while others do not. Fortunately, most people can improve their resilience by practicing any or all of these strategies in ordinary, low-stress situations.

VULNERABILITY TO STRESS: RISK FACTORS

Just as certain characteristics, perspectives, and skills help to enhance resilience and performance, others may tend to make you more vulnerable to stress. Most of these risk factors can be seen as opposites of the resilience attributes listed above. Risk factors include social isolation, low self-esteem, poor communication skills, problem avoidance, pessimistic outlook, inactivity, intellectual rigidity, unrealistic expectations, absence of control, history of anxiety or depression, and the inability or unwillingness to seek help when needed. Understand these risk factors and do something to manage or counteract them. Build a social support network of family, friends, neighbors, or church members. Talk with them and realistically assess what you should do, what you can do, and whom you can rely on for help when needed. Have a plan in place or at least talk in advance with those whose support you might eventually need. For example, have a conversation with siblings about how best to manage things if one of your parents falls ill or must be hospitalized when you are stationed elsewhere or deployed overseas.

Individuals who have a history of untreated depression, alcoholism or substance abuse, childhood physical and/or sexual abuse, or a family history of anxiety disorder are also at increased risk for severe immediate or lasting negative effects of stress or stress-related disorders such as PTSD. If any of these risk factors apply to you, it would be smart to request additional guidance from a trusted health care professional sooner rather than later, before you are exposed to the stress of combat. Use the chain of command, a chaplain, or others not in the medical system if you feel more comfortable doing so. It is not a sign of weakness to discuss your concerns in confidence with a trusted person. If you are at risk for stress-related difficulties, it is responsible to prepare in any way you can to better handle unexpected or extreme stress.

HARDINESS

Psychological stability and resilience to stress have been linked to a personality characteristic known as hardiness, which is usually associated with three fundamental attitudes or orientations. Hardy individuals successfully adapt to and manage difficult situations by approaching them with commitment, a sense of control, and a perspective on difficulty as challenge. They often view potentially stressful problems as opportunities for growth and development.

Commitment. Philosopher Friedrich Nietzsche wisely observed "He who has a *why* to live for can bear with almost any *how.*" Nowhere is this more obvious than in the warfighter's service to his or her country. Members of the U.S. military are usually motivated by a very strong sense of commitment. They have a notable allegiance to and involvement in their work-related situations and relationships. They express their pride and demonstrate loyalty to friends and coworkers. They genuinely believe that their work is meaningful. These characteristics are typical of the hardy personality. Because hardy individuals are motivated by commitment to a purpose greater than themselves, they are better able to keep their individual struggles and job-related stress in perspective.

Control. Central to the hardy personality is a positive orientation toward active problem solving, simply described as a sense of control. If you have a strong sense

> ### DEALING WITH STRESS: FOUR SIMPLE STRATEGIES
>
> 1. Keep problems in perspective. Remind yourself that things could be worse. Be thankful for what's good in your life.
> 2. Consider your past success. You have overcome stress in the past. You are stronger for it now. You've done it before. You can do it again.
> 3. Focus on your sense of purpose. Your work has meaning. You are dedicated to your work.
> 4. Practice psychological self-discipline. Interrupt negative thoughts with positive thoughts. Remember that stress is temporary. Think about your long-term goals.

of control, you tend to believe that you can take action to effectively influence your surroundings, work hard to produce good outcomes, creatively solve problems, and persevere to overcome difficulties. Although biology and genes prob-

A soldier wearing the Land Warrior system moves through a courtyard in Sukkaryiah in the Sulah ad Dihn Province of Iraq. *Photo courtesy of the U.S. Army/Capt. Richard Ybarra*

ably influence this and other important personality characteristics, research in this area also indicates that we can continue to learn and develop our sense of control throughout our lives by effort and experience. With each new accomplishment and achievement, we gain confidence in ourselves and in our ability to overcome new challenges. The greater our sense of control, the less vulnerable we are to stress. Here again, by working to meet individual goals and reach new milestones, you can improve your resilience to stress.

Challenge. Hardy individuals view problems not as threats but as challenges. They view virtually every situation, good or bad, as a valuable opportunity to learn and improve by experience. By attaching meaning and benefit to hardship, the hardy individual engages his or her own other hardy characteristics (commitment, control) toward active involvement in finding solutions.

This determined ability to see positive potential in adversity allows the hardy warfighter to build on his or her existing skills, knowledge, experience, and effectiveness. For reasons considered earlier in this chapter, it can also provide an essential psychological buffer against an intense and potentially problematic physiological response to stress.

Commitment, control, and challenge orientations interact as complementary and synergistic components of the hardy personality. The individual who finds meaning and challenge in difficulty will tend to develop a greater commitment and seek to exert control or participate directly in problem solving. Likewise, individuals who participate actively will tend to develop a greater sense of impact and commitment to cause. As you actively encourage or develop any one or two of these approaches to difficulty, you will enjoy the beneficial effects of them all and thereby improve your personal hardiness to stress. What's more, you may be able to encourage others to similar benefit. By demonstrating that you view difficulties as challenges, and by actively working to solve problems constructively, you exercise leadership and serve by example. Those who observe your approach may wish to emulate it. A goal-oriented sense of unit cohesion and confidence will increase morale, enhance operational effectiveness, and ultimately improve your odds of survival on and off the battlefield.

As a final note on the subject of hardiness, it is important to add that commitment to a larger purpose can also play an important role in motivating personal conviction and individual achievement. As a member of the military, you know that when you improve yourself as an individual, you also improve your value and effectiveness as a warfighter. What you might not know is that by pursuing your individual goals, you are also buffering yourself from negative effects of stress. The harder and more consistently you work toward clearly defined goals and personal achievements, the more you condition your body and mind to tolerate physical and psychological stress.

Just as you can improve your physical endurance by running each day, you can improve your stress endurance by setting goals and engaging yourself in the effort to meet them. Improved psychological endurance may also make operational challenges and difficulties seem less daunting and more easily overcome by perseverance.

THE FAITH FACTOR

For many, confidence, meaning, and perspective are supported by faith in a higher power or purpose. Such faith usually stems from deeply held spiritual beliefs that inspire trust, courage, and hope. Faith might reflect belief in a higher power, commitment to a particular set of ethical or moral principles, a view of the world itself and/or a sense of place within it. Or faith may not be a part of your life at all.

SEAL students participate in Log PT (physical training). Log PT is a demonstration of physical strength, endurance, and the importance of teamwork. *U.S. Navy photo by Photographer's Mate 2nd Class Eric S. Logsdon*

A moment to relax and reflect during a long day of flight deck operations aboard the USS Abraham Lincoln, conducting combat operations in support of Operation Enduring Freedom and Southern Watch. *U.S. Navy photo by Photographer's Mate Airman Philip A. McDaniel*

Whatever its source or description, faith provides a framework that helps some people make meaning of the events in their lives and in the world around them. This is especially helpful when we confront moments that might otherwise seem inexplicably tragic, pointless, or hopeless. Because faith helps some to interpret their experiences and shape their behavior, it can be very valuable as a buffer against the negative effects of traumatic stress. People who have the faith factor believe they are better equipped to adapt to trauma if they can draw upon deeply held religious, spiritual, or ethical belief systems. Although beliefs might initially be shaken by traumatic stress, doubt provides opportunity for growth. By additional thought and exploration, some are even able to develop their faith and find it stronger in the end. For some individuals, faith itself is born of the need to overcome trauma and find meaning in survival. For others, meaning can be constructed in other ways, and many people who have no spiritual beliefs or faith are able to cope quite successfully with stress.

Fellowship in faith can help unite and support soldiers, especially those with similar beliefs. However, religious insensitivity can also divide and even alienate those who hold different beliefs or none at all. If faith is a part of your life, it can be a bulwark for you in difficult times. If it is not, you may find your strength in other areas of life. American military personnel can be proud to serve a nation that protects all possible choices that individuals may make when it comes to faith.

BUILDING RESILIENCE

As you read the preceding paragraphs, you probably recognized certain traits, dispositions, and types of behavior as typical of you or someone you know. Resilience is not a new idea or attribute. It rings familiar because it describes something most of us already know how to be and how to do. The challenge is to sustain and improve upon the resilient characteristics and strategies we already possess. If you can develop your resilience as a habit—as an ordinary way of living—it will come more naturally to you when you need it most.

You can develop your own resilience by practicing any or all of the following strategies:

- Set realistic expectations for yourself and others.
- Think about positive results of change.
- Learn new skills. Seek new knowledge.

- Try new ways of doing familiar tasks. Practice flexibility.
- Apply your strengths creatively.
- Acknowledge your weaknesses and look for ways to improve.
- Envision yourself in new situations. Imagine positive outcomes.
- Encourage others to succeed.
- Nurture supportive relationships with family, friends, and colleagues.
- Ask for help when needed.
- Get regular exercise.
- Get and/or stay involved in social activities.
- Practice your faith.
- Spend time with people who make you laugh.
- Be honest with others when you are stressed. Ask for their patience and support.
- Think about how far you have come and take pride in your accomplishments.
- Set goals for the future and take clear, manageable steps to reach them.

Even in a combat theater, boredom can be a significant source of stress. Many troops deal with boredom by setting and working toward personal physical goals, taking correspondence courses, working on creative projects (e.g., videos, photography), or writing. These types of activities are helpful to preserve a sense of meaning, progress, productivity, and substance during down times.

RESILIENT BEHAVIOR: MANAGING STRESS

When no amount of preparation or personality is enough to prevent stress or protect you from it, the best you can do is to find or design strategies to help you live with stress. Such strategies might include regular exercise, meditation, hobbies, writing, pharmaceutical support (on the advice of a physician only), or other activities found to be helpful on an individual basis. Managing stress doesn't alleviate the source of the stress but can help you reduce or control stress-related symptoms and problems.

It is an unavoidable part of being human that sooner or later, each of us will encounter a situation or event that forces us to acknowledge stress and manage it. At any given time, most people are managing multiple sources of mild to moderate stress in their daily lives. Some people manage stress more elegantly or effectively than others. How well you manage stress can be judged by your ability to overcome its negative effects and perform effectively.

A Marine Corps sergeant plays her guitar after working hours. *U.S. Navy photo by Mass Communication Specialist 3rd Class Daniel Barker*

Stress management can be seen as a battle of sorts. Effective battle planning should involve thoughtful review of strengths, weaknesses, and lessons learned. Effective stress management requires preparation and honest self-awareness. If you are willing and able to acknowledge your personal strengths and weaknesses—including your past mistakes, your sore spots, your issues, your limitations, your vulnerabilities—you can make more appropriate and effective choices about what strategies might be most helpful to you when you confront stressful situations. Consider your past experiences as well as current stresses in your life. What strategies have been helpful or harmful in the past? What have you learned from your mistakes? Do you know other people who seem to be very good at managing stress and, if so, what strategies do they employ? Might those same strategies be helpful to you? Why or why not?

The purpose of a having a plan is to be prepared before you find yourself in a crisis situation. You should develop your individualized plan when you are relaxed and your mind is undistracted by stress. First, think about specific strategies that have worked well for you in the past. Think about the situations in which you used these strategies, and why. Did these strategies feel comfortable to you? Did you make a conscious choice to use certain strategies, or did you simply fall back on them because you didn't know what else to do? If you had had more time to think about it, might you have chosen a different strategy? Would some other strategy be more effective in a different situation? For example, a regular exercise program may have helped you to manage the stress of unemployment or divorce, but suppose you suffered a physical injury that prevented you from engaging in regular exercise. How might you then manage the stress of physical disability? As you begin to develop a better understanding of your own stress management style or approach, it will become easier to identify multiple and contingency strategies for dealing with unique or unexpected situations. A strong plan should include multiple strategies, options, and backup plans in case your first-choice strategies become impossible or ineffective. In every case, ask yourself if your plan will honor and preserve your relationships with the people who matter most to you. If a particular strategy would tend to distance you from family or friends, it is probably a bad choice. Likewise, avoid strategies, such as alcohol consumption, that might complicate an already stressful situation or cause additional problems.

In addition to the obvious benefit of preparation, the process of developing a stress management plan can itself be a very useful exercise. For example, you may discover a new sense of control as you find that you can make proactive choices about how you will respond and deal with stress. Gradually, stress may begin to seem less like a threat and more like a challenge. Once you have a plan for managing stress, you can put it to the test as a means to manage the big and little stresses of everyday life. Think of these experiences as field exercises. By practicing your plan—and by refining and improving it as necessary—you may begin to see stress as an opportunity to build on your strengths and correct for your weaknesses. All of these perspectives and orientations are associated with improved resilience to stress. In short, you may enhance your overall resilience to stress simply by planning for how to manage it.

MANAGING YOUR MIND UNDER STRESS

The Greek Stoic philosopher Epictetus once observed, "Men are disturbed not by things, but by the views which they take of them." Certainly, the human mind can be very creative in its perceptions of reality. This is not always a good or healthy thing. For example, some people cope with stress by denying that it exists or that it bothers them. Although this approach may provide some temporary sense of comfort, it is ultimately counterproductive because it avoids the need for real solutions to real problems. To effectively manage your own mental response to stress, you must first recognize and accept the reality of stress and its natural impact on the human body and mind. Then and only then can you effectively leverage the power of your own mind to enhance your resilience to stress and your ability to manage its effects.

WAYS OF THINKING

It is well-worn advice because it works: when you are dealing with stress, it helps to keep the problem(s) in perspective. By exercising our powers of comparison, we can diminish the power of stressful situations and events. Put simply, it does help to look on the bright side. Likewise, it may be helpful to practice gratitude. Consider the many things for which you are thankful, the ways in which you consider yourself to be fortunate, and the circumstances in which you find some comfort. By urging your mind toward a positive perspective and hopeful orientation, you can weaken the negative cycle of fear and anxiety that may interfere with problem solving.

Another powerful strategy for dealing with stress is to consider past successes. This can help to focus and improve your confidence and will also serve to remind you that your current difficulties are temporary.

Certainly, you have overcome other stressful experiences in your life. Try to recall moments when you doubted your ability to endure or move ahead. For example, you may have doubted your ability to

---

WRITING WHAT'S WRONG . . .

Many people find it helpful to write about their experiences. The process of writing can help you to analyze, interpret, and reestablish your sense of control over difficult memories and experiences.

Focus on big picture questions:

✓ What have you learned?
✓ Could your experience help you in the future?
✓ How has your experience changed you?
✓ What is the most constructive path toward recovery?
✓ What do you feel you need most today?
✓ What will you need in the future?
✓ When do you imagine yourself feeling better?
✓ Can you put your experience to good use, such as helping or teaching others?

survive boot camp. Now you know that your worst fears were unfounded. You did endure, you did survive, and you are stronger today as a result. The difficulties you faced then were real but temporary. By overcoming those difficulties, you took a step toward long-term goals. You can see now how the stress of boot camp was necessary in order to meet long-term goals. You were capable then, and you are even more capable now. Put yesterday's success to work for you as motivation, reassurance, and inspiration in the present. Remember too that you are well trained to do your job. Trust your training and exercise your confidence.

Some people carry "battle chips" or charms and use personal rituals that provide a quick sense of calm or comfort in the midst of stress. Many warfighters find it helpful to carry a photo, coin, or some other special reminder of hope. This strategy should not be based in superstition, for charms and rituals obviously do not provide good luck or magical protection from bullets and bombs. But for many individuals, stress can be relieved, if only for a moment, by pausing briefly to connect with a positive feeling, memory, or idea.

MANAGING YOUR BODY UNDER STRESS

At the beginning of this chapter, we presented essential information about how the human body's sympathetic nervous system responds to stress. The body's response is oriented to immediate survival, but it can, in certain situations, overwhelm the mind and interfere with good decision-making. There are specific strategies you can use on a regular basis to engage your body's own (parasympathetic nervous system) ability to achieve and maintain a balanced response to stress and to recover from its own stress response.

Breathing. The first and fastest thing you can do to manage your response to stress is to change how you breathe. Different breathing techniques may be more or less useful in different situations. Find a technique that works for you and practice three times a day for several minutes. Breathing techniques are also a useful way to relax during down times or just before sleeping.

Progressive muscle relaxation. When you are under stress, your muscles will tend to contract. Over time, you may adapt to this and be unaware of the persistent tension in your muscles. When you are trying to manage stress, it is helpful to relieve your body of muscle tension. Tensing and then relaxing each muscle group in your body can do this. Begin at one end of your body (feet and legs) and methodically work your way toward the other end (shoulders and neck).

Visual imagery. Many people find it physically relaxing to practice visual imagery. This is similar to meditation but with a specific focus on finding a place of comfort and relaxation. If you have practiced visual imagery on a regular basis, you can go to your chosen place of relaxation more quickly to find immediate relief from stress.

You should also be aware that good habits and health are important to the effective management of your body's response to stress. If your body is tired or out of balance, its response to unexpected stress may be more extreme or difficult to manage. Adequate sleep, healthy diet, regular exercise, and physical recreation all are important to maintaining a healthy balance between body and mind.

LIFE AND DEATH

Military service is an opportunity to play a role, perhaps even a heroic role, in history. It also raises the very real possibility that you may be exposed to life-or-death situations. You may see other human beings suffer serious injuries or be killed. They may be civilians. They may be your buddies. You may have to kill other human beings. The remainder of this chapter provides information drawn from the experiences of other warfighters who have faced these and related challenges. This information includes straightforward recognition of normal and sometimes difficult emotional reactions.

KILLING

The specific psychological and emotional effects of killing certainly can be different for each person and circumstance. Don't be surprised if you experience an

---

DEEP BREATHING

Deep breathing is a simple, effective way to intervene directly in your body's stress response and keep stress-related physiological responses under control. This technique helps lower blood pressure and reduce anxiety. The objective is to breathe slowly and deeply, taking about six breaths per minute. (Normal breathing rate is around 15–20 breaths per minute.)

Technique
Place one hand on your abdomen, about an inch above your navel. Inhale slowly through your nose, counting to four, drawing the air deep into your body, below your chest. You should feel your hand move as your abdomen expands outward. Hold the breath for a count of four. Exhale slowly through your mouth, again counting to four. With each breath, concentrate on the flow of air and its sensation as it enters and exits your body. Feel your hand move as your abdomen expands outward and inward with each breath. Pause for a count of four between breaths. Repeat for 5–10 minutes.

If your mind wanders to stressful thoughts, focus on specific words or sentences while breathing. For example, think of the word "cool" or say to yourself, "I am beginning to feel cool" very slowly as you inhale, and "relax" or "I am beginning to feel relaxed" very slowly as you exhale.

You can combine the basic deep breathing exercise with relaxing images. For example, imagine that you are surrounded by a cool, damp fog of refreshing and relaxing moisture. As you inhale, imagine that this fog slowly enters your body to relax you. As you exhale, the fog soaks up stress and takes it away.

PROGRESSIVE MUSCLE RELAXATION

Stress causes muscles to contract. You can relieve this effect by training your muscles to relax.

Technique
Tighten each muscle group for five seconds (counting one-thousand, one-thousand-one, one-thousand-two, etc.). Then relax the same group of muscles for five seconds. Repeat twice. Move on to the next muscle group, progressing gradually from one end of your body to the other.

Hands. Place your hands as fists and raise them to chest level. Hold, relax, and repeat.

Forearms. First, place your arms at your sides. Raise your forearms and bend your wrists downward, tightening the forearm muscles for five seconds. Relax for five seconds and repeat.

Biceps. Raise your arms to shoulder level and assume the bicep pose (forearms raised, biceps tightened). Hold, relax, and repeat.

Shoulders. Raise your shoulders as if shrugging, as high as possible. Hold, relax, and repeat.

Stomach. Pull in and tighten your torso as if you were doing a sit-up. Hold, relax, and repeat.

Thighs. While seated, press the soles of your feet against the ground to create tension in your thigh muscles. Hold, relax, and repeat.

Calves. While lying down, raise your feet three inches off the ground, bending your toes up and toward your torso as far as you can. Hold, relax, and repeat.

Feet. Curl your toes as though you were trying to squeeze mud through them. Hold, relax, and repeat.

Practice the entire technique twice. Take your time—you are training your body to relax. With practice, you will find that your body will relax more quickly. Eventually, you may achieve the same whole-body effect by relaxing just one or two muscle groups.

initial sense of exhilaration when you realize you have killed an enemy combatant. In the immediate context of combat, you are keenly aware of the need to survive. Your body's stress response includes an adrenaline surge that might make you feel high. You might also feel an initial sense of relief in knowing that you were able to do what was necessary. However, even in the context of combat, the act of killing can also be quite stressful.

On a personal level, the act of killing another human being is always significant. Even when you know you did what had to be done, it may be difficult to kill another person without feeling that you have done something wrong. At some point, you might recall your initial sense of excitement and be disturbed or confused by it. Some people experience feelings of guilt, remorse, regret, or even trauma. Others do not.

Recognize that while you may have unexpected feelings about killing, your reaction is understandable. Ultimately, it may be necessary to accept the permanence of lingering doubts, remorse, or guilt. Talking with others can help to clear confusion and focus your mind on rational acceptance. In particular, you should request help as soon as possible if you experience problems such as persistent feelings of uneasiness, overwhelming sense of remorse, loss of appetite, loss of interest, or difficulty sleeping.

DEATH

The suddenness of death can be shocking, even in war. Those who die in war are not always combatants and enemies. Sometimes they are civilians caught in the crossfire. Sometimes they are children. Sometimes they are your friends.

When you witness the death of another human being, your initial reaction may be one of relief. Surrounded by the violence of war, you are thankful to have survived the moment. This first reaction might be followed by other feelings, including guilt, self-blame, helplessness, and loss of confidence in your ability to protect yourself and others. Some people experience survivor's guilt, wishing they had died in place of someone else. The best time to deal with such feelings is as soon as possible by discussing your experience with a trusted friend, leader, or mental health officer. It might be helpful to honor a fallen comrade by escorting the body home. You can express your support for the families of those who have lost their lives and offer to participate in funeral proceedings. Family members will usually appreciate any information you can share about your experiences with their lost loved one. The process of sharing experiences and memories can be very helpful for all concerned.

VISUAL IMAGERY

Visual imagery is a simple technique. It provides an imaginary place of relaxation. With practice, you can find this place quickly. One advantage of the visual imagery technique is that you can practice it almost anywhere simply by closing your eyes. It will not be obvious to observers that you are doing anything but resting your eyes.

Technique
Imagine that you are moving—floating or riding—forward into the distance ahead of you. First, you can barely see your point of destination. As you draw nearer, you begin to see objects such as trees, rocks, vegetation, water, etc. Imagine how these things smell. Is there a breeze? Do you hear noises, such as birds chirping or tree branches moving? Bring all of your senses into this process. Consider the temperature of your surroundings. Invent in your mind the sights, smells, and conditions that would make you comfortable. You might see mountains on the horizon, or perhaps the ocean shore. Include whatever landscape or features you appreciate as beautiful or relaxing. Then stop and enjoy being in this place. Stay in this place for a while, for as long as you can or for as long as you must. Let your mind wander. Just relax.

When it is time to leave your place of relaxation, imagine your favorite form of transportation for your return. Imagine this journey as clearly as you can. When you have returned, open your eyes gently. Remember that you can go back to your place of relaxation as often as you like.

Some people find that after practicing visual imagery several times, they can achieve a similar effect by looking at a photograph of such a place. They have trained their bodies to relax quickly by quick visual reference to a place that reminds them of their original relaxation experience.

CRITICAL INCIDENT DEBRIEFING

The purpose of critical incident debriefing is to provide accurate information and useful support

A U.S. Air Force staff sergeant pays his respects during a ceremony to recognize fallen security forces airmen. *U.S. Air Force Photo/Senior Airman Levi Riendeau*

to those who have been exposed to extremely stressful or potentially traumatic events. Events of this kind might include training accidents resulting in death, unit suicides, or aviation mishaps. Typically, a critical incident debriefing will include all personnel who were directly involved or familiar with the incident in question. A critical incident debriefing is not a formal investigation. Nor does it assume that those who attend are vulnerable to psychological distress. If you are asked to attend a debriefing, it is not because someone questions your ability to cope. Rather, it is because you have important information or perspective that may be helpful to others and because you are a part of the group that has been affected by or involved in the event. The point of this effort is to provide everyone involved with the benefit of access to relevant facts and accurate information.

Critical incident debriefing is not a waste of time. On the contrary, by hearing and sharing the facts of the experience, you will be better able to evaluate the incident for yourself.

After reconstructing an event by reviewing the facts and individual experiences, you will be provided with guidance concerning what you might expect to feel in the short term and how best to deal with it. You will be given information to help you identify problems in yourself or others. Even if you feel confident in your own ability to cope with the incident, remember that the information you receive at the debriefing can prepare you to help a friend who may find it more difficult. When handled effectively, critical incident debriefing prevents misinformation and promotes cohesion.

CONCLUSION

Military culture embraces challenge, hardship, sacrifice, and even a certain amount of suffering. Lifelong bonds are often formed among service members who have endured hardship together. Hardship is no small part of what makes military service so meaningful. In this context, some might feel that concerns about stress effects and stress-related disorders are a sign of weakness. It may be important here to recognize that stress need not be—and cannot be—entirely eliminated or avoided. Like sleep and food, stress can be seen as a necessary, understandable, and manageable part of the military experience. Like fatigue and nutritional imbalance, stress can also have overwhelming effects that threaten job performance and well-being.

When stress is problematic, it is important to know you can seek help without fear of judgment, criticism, or ridicule. It is a sign of strength to seek help when needed. It shows that you recognize the need to preserve your status as a healthy, effective, and reliable military professional. The goal of this chapter has been to offer a healthy perspective on stress, improve your understanding of how your body responds to stress, and show how this might affect your performance. In the next chapter, we will consider the types of demands and sources of stress that you are likely to confront as a member of the modern military.

CHAPTER FOUR

Surviving and Thriving in Combat

Prior to the Gulf War in 1990–1991, the U.S. military was preoccupied primarily with the Cold War and related contingency operations. Our guiding strategy was to establish and maintain a stable balance of forces to prevent direct nuclear conflict between the United States and the Soviet Union. During this period, members of the U.S. armed services enjoyed a certain amount of stability and predictability in their military service. For many, it was possible to time occasional overseas deployments to coincide with favorable family circumstances. Service members who were assigned to long tours could often be accompanied by their families. Spanning several decades, the Cold War provided a fairly predictable context in which to live and serve as a member of the U.S. military.

Some of that stability has been lost. So-called contingency operations are limited in scope and duration. They are short-term operations that occur unexpectedly, such as interventions in Haiti, Panama, Somalia, and, on a much larger scale, Kuwait (Operation Desert Storm). Contingency operations may involve a broad spectrum of combat conditions, including conventional combined-arms combat, support, or stability operations. Because they are often sudden and sometimes intense, such operations can be very stressful for affected service members and their families. However, this impact is usually fairly limited in its duration and extent. Because contingency operations are typically focused on very specific objectives in unique circumstances, they usually involve a relatively limited number of military units and personnel.

The first decade of the twenty-first century has been characterized by much larger and longer commitments of American forces. Active and reserve service members have endured lengthy and repeated deployments as needed to support a complicated variety of mission requirements. While there is no immediately apparent prospect of returning to Cold War-like conditions, no one knows what the future may hold. Soldiers must be mentally prepared for the possibility that our nation could become involved in a variety of conflicts, different types of which may make very different demands on them and their families.

The wars in Iraq and Afghanistan have challenged our military establishment both by the magnitude and duration of the troop commitments required and by the nature of the conflict itself. Military units and members have been called upon to adapt to new roles and requirements that are less focused on conventional combat and driven more by the tenets of emerging counterinsurgency doctrine. Military members today are serving at a point of transition in our national history; we are not certain what the trajectory of military transformation will be or what challenges our military will face in the future. But military members are likely to continue to be tested as severely as any soldiers in history.

The conditions of modern war are challenging, but practical information from the field of psychology can help you understand and manage your natural reactions to the situations you may face. In the context of current conflicts, it may be especially helpful to consider some of the unique challenges inherent in modern warfare:

- Cultural differences and our attitudes about other people
- Dealing with insurgency and insurgents
- The impact of aggression, abuse, and dehumanization

TABLE 4.1

Cold War	Contingency Operations	Vietnam War / Iraq War
Long (decades)	Short (days-months)	Long (years)
Expected large, force-on-force, combined-arms conflict	Scope varies (e.g., Gulf War, Panama)	Large-scale operations
Conventional war	Conventional or SASO*	Conventional and SASO
Demands were high but stable	Demands unpredictable but brief	Demands high, unpredictable, and long
* SASO (Stability and Support Operations) includes peace operations, security assistance, foreign internal defense (helping governments maintain order against insurgencies), counterterrorism and counterdrug operations, domestic and/or foreign support in times of natural or environmental disasters, and humanitarian assistance.		

Each of these can complicate individual psychological responses to war. Each will be addressed in practical terms within this chapter.

Finally, it is important to remember that in addition to military conflict, members of the U.S. armed services may also be called upon to support domestic emergency management efforts. Although such needs have usually been met through the support of the National Guard, we must recognize that the future is uncertain with respect to natural disasters and the global war on terror. Future direct attacks on U.S. territory are certainly possible. In 2005 the devastating impact of Hurricane Katrina showed that nature has the potential to wreak havoc on a scale that requires a coordinated response from civilian and military agencies and personnel. In situations of this type, service members may encounter many of the same stresses that are common in constabulary operations.

CULTURAL DIFFERENCES

As human beings, we tend to be most comfortable with what is familiar. We like what we know. Psychological research has shown that it is natural for human beings to feel relaxed, content, and safe in familiar surroundings. When we live and work in our own culture, we know what to expect and, in general, what others expect from us. For the most part, we feel we can identify situations and people who pose a possible threat to our safety. We know how to locate goods and services. We know how to behave in public.

Unfamiliar situations and cultures can make us feel insecure, frustrated, lost, and sometimes even angry. Ordinary citizens may experience these difficulties in foreign countries where they are welcome as tourists. Therefore, you should not be surprised if you feel stressed when you have been deployed to an unfamiliar country or culture where U.S. military intervention may or may not be welcome. Feelings of isolation and insecurity are simply an unavoidable fact of life in new and unfamiliar settings. Remember too that even those who welcome your presence may also feel confused or threatened by your unfamiliar expectations and behavior.

Military life provides a culture of its own, and this may help you to maintain your sense of orientation and belonging even when you find yourself in otherwise unfamiliar settings. Psychologists have found that as we become more familiar with other cultures and citizens, we grow more comfortable and begin to regain our sense of control. By making an effort to learn the language and respect the customs of different cultures, you can connect with its people in a way

Army and Air Force members of a provincial reconstruction team stretch with children from the local community before playing soccer in Jalalabad, Afghanistan. *U.S. Air Force photo/Staff Sgt. Joshua T. Jasper*

that will help you to better understand and value your experience. Perhaps more importantly, it may be essential to mission success that you be able to establish such connections with local citizens.

It is important to remember that you do not have to accept or approve of others' customs in order to acknowledge and respect them. You can behave respectfully toward others even if you find their ways distasteful or difficult to understand. As a member of the U.S. military, it is your responsibility to do no less. The success of your mission may depend upon it.

INSURGENCY AND INSURGENTS

Sometimes our enemies are uniformed soldiers, easily recognized, organized, and regulated by military training and codes of conduct. When you engage in combat against uniformed soldiers, you can easily identify them as the "enemy." You recognize the difference between opposing military forces and their civilian, noncombatant counterparts. Because you are a soldier yourself, you can understand the actions of opponent soldiers as legitimate and expected.

The situation becomes much more complicated, challenging, and frustrating in conflicts that involve insurgency. The strategy of the insurgent fighter is to

A U.S. Navy hospitalman examines a local Afghani at a temporary medical clinic in the Farah Province. *U.S. Marine Corps photo by Cpl. Jason T. Guiliano*

appear as an ordinary civilian, attack without warning, and disappear just as quickly. By melting back into the civilian population, insurgents are able to avoid discovery and escape retaliation. Often, insurgent attacks defy even the most universally held codes of military conduct. The resulting psychological effects of insurgent attacks may be nearly as damaging as their physical impact. Insurgents frustrate our natural human desire to organize our experiences in a sensible way. We perceive insurgent attacks as unfair and dishonorable.

Insurgencies make it impossible to tell the difference between combatants and noncombatants. When we can't tell the difference between fighters and civilians, we naturally begin to generalize our suspicions across the entire population. Unfortunately, this makes it more difficult to win the trust, faith, and goodwill of civilians who might otherwise be supportive and helpful. If we behave in ways that unnecessarily frighten civilians or seem careless of their safety, we may be playing into the hands of the insurgents. Such a situation is complicated and often frustrating. It may be helpful to seek guidance from leaders and fellow soldiers who have had more time on the ground to gain a sense of how best to manage the situation. Insurgency is an inherently psychological form of warfare. As a soldier, you must learn to anticipate, recognize, and manage the

Soldiers of the 1st Cavalry Division prepare to enter a dwelling while on patrol in Iraq. *Photo courtesy of the U.S. Army*

psychological effects of this type of warfare on you and the people with whom you interact.

AGGRESSION, ABUSE, AND DEHUMANIZATION

Psychological research has helped us better understand many of the social and psychological conditions that promote aggression, violence, and abuse. If you are able to anticipate and recognize these conditions and understand their potential impact, you will find it easier to maintain high standards of behavior based on your training and core values.

Frustration can lead to aggression. Extreme frustration can provoke aggressive thoughts and feelings. However, as a soldier, you must not use your power, skills and abilities, or weapons as means to relieve personal frustration. Vigorous exercise is a better way to blow off steam in a safe, healthy, and acceptable way.

Discomfort can lead to resentment. After any length of time spent living and working in harsh conditions, you may find yourself feeling impatient with others and resentful of those who enjoy better conditions. Remind yourself that discomfort is temporary and your fellow soldiers are feeling it too.

Isolation can lead to aberrant behavior. Life in a combat zone is very different than life in any other circumstance, situation, or environment. New and difficult situations can exert powerful influences upon how we think, feel, and behave. It is important to remember that although you must confront a host of new demands and difficulties, you are still you. You should continue to behave according to the same high standards that guided your life and service prior to deployment. Remember that you are a military professional and you represent the United States.

Grief and loss can lead to anger. If you witness the injury or death of friends, you may experience feelings of anger or hatred toward the enemy. Such feelings are normal, but it is important that you manage your behavior in a professional way that is consistent with your training and with the high standards of your position as a representative of the U.S. military.

Stereotypes are dangerous. "The enemy" is a threatening entity that must be weakened or eliminated. However, when taken to the extreme, labeling can be abused as propaganda to stereotype and dehumanize entire populations. Derogatory terms are often used to invoke stereotypes. It is important to understand that derogatory terms are not harmless nicknames. Rather, they reinforce negative stereotypes, devalue human life, and ultimately endanger all of us. As a human being and as a soldier, you should resist the urge to stereotype other human beings and understand that the success of your mission may depend upon recognizing the value and dignity of all peoples.

It is a common assumption that how we behave is the direct result of what we think and believe. Interestingly, psychological research shows that the opposite is often true. In fact, we often change our minds and attitudes to match our behavior and the behavior of those around us. For this reason among others, it is important to maintain good habits of speech and conduct. Your own good behavior will help to reinforce the positive principles you know are right for you and for others. If you choose instead to go along with others' questionable language or conduct, you start down a slippery slope that can quickly erode your basic sense of right and wrong.

DEPLOYMENT TO COMBAT

During World War II, American soldiers knew that their deployment would continue for the duration of the war. They didn't know how long the war might last, but for most of those who served during World War II, combat service could be seen as a unique and temporary circumstance, a one-time hardship from which they would eventually return to resume their normal civilian lives. Today, our military is an all-volunteer force with very different expectations and requirements. Repeated deployments have become the norm for full-time active and reserve service members. The current deployment cycle places significant and repetitive burdens on all service members. Adequate preparation is essential for soldiers and their families, all of whom confront and must learn to cope with many stressful realities and uncertainties. Some of these challenges are also discussed in Chapter 1 of this book.

It is normal to experience conflicting emotions about impending deployment, especially if you will be sent into a combat zone. You may feel a sense of excitement in knowing that you will play an active role in events of national and historical significance. Combat duty is the real deal—it provides an opportunity for you to test yourself and your training and to face difficult challenges in the company of others with whom you have already built strong relationships of trust and respect.

On the other hand, you may also feel anxious and perhaps even fearful. You may wonder if you are up to the task. You may worry about how your loved ones will manage in your absence. Most service members experience some or all of these feelings and concerns at one time or another. Remind yourself that the overwhelming majority of service members do eventually return home from combat to find that their worst fears were unfounded.

The best way to feel prepared is to get prepared. If you have not already served in combat, talk with others who have. Learn from their experiences. Seek people and resources to review your skills and focus your attention on the job at hand. The Center for Army Lessons Learned (CALL) has published a book entitled *Soldiers' Handbook: The First 100 Days* (No. 07-15), which offers a concise summary of essential lessons and guidance from veterans of recent conflicts.

Many of the resilience strategies outlined in Chapter 3 of this book can be very useful in supporting a positive outlook and successful orientation to deployment. For example, it is reasonable to expect that deployment will bring change. It is helpful to think in advance about the potential positive results of your deployment, including any new skills and knowledge you might gain and how these benefits can be put to positive use for you and your family. If you think of deployment as an opportunity for experience and growth, you can better imagine and shape positive outcomes. Set goals in advance and know that you will take pride in new accomplishments.

Another way to prepare for deployment is to focus on your motivations to serve as a member of the military. These include your commitment to freedom and justice, your dedication to service, and perhaps also a strong desire to live and work with others who hold these same ideals. On a more practical level, you might also be motivated by educational and/or financial considerations. Finally, on a personal level, you might simply enjoy the challenges, satisfaction, and personal and professional relationships that you experience during your military career.

It may also be helpful to explore and discuss your motivations openly and honestly with friends and family members. This type of discussion provides you an opportunity to acknowledge the hardships and implications of your work and in turn provides others an opportunity to express their support, accept hardships, and share information that may assist you in reaching difficult decisions.

FAMILY AND FRIENDS

Whether you are married or unmarried, with children or not, you have family members and friends who care about your well-being. Certainly, you feel a sense of obligation to your loved ones. You want to be there for them. At the same time, you feel a need to be there for your country and your comrades. Your sense of obligation may, at times, seem to compete with itself. If you are fortunate enough to be able to exercise some degree of control over your military assignments, you may feel guilty when you seek or accept assignments that involve separation from family.

Similarly, you may fear that you are failing your buddies or jeopardizing your unit if you choose to be reassigned or retire so that you can better support your family's needs. You might even feel resentment toward family members or colleagues whose needs or demands present an impossible dilemma.

Although the stresses associated with deployment are certainly real and often complicated, there are actions you can take to reduce the impact of separation on yourself and others. First and foremost, let your family and friends know what you are thinking and how you are feeling. Communication is important to the quality of human relationships. In times of uncertainty, communication may be nothing less than essential to the survival of your closest relationships with other people.

Talk to your loved ones and listen to their concerns. Work hard to understand what they think and feel. Try to remember that fear can cause frustration, which may be expressed in terms that sound like anger.

Do your best to anticipate issues and problems that may arise during your absence. If you can plan in advance how to manage difficult situations, you will feel more confident and less stressed if or when the time comes to deal with them.

Build trust by talking in advance about what might happen and discussing potential responses to difficult events. Misunderstanding can lead to mistrust.

Build networks of friends and family members who can be ready quickly to provide help as needed. You know that you depend upon and value the support you derive from relationships with your fellow service members. Realize that you, your family, and your friends can form equally valuable relationships to facilitate coping with stress in your absence.

Thanks to modern communications technologies, today's soldiers can stay in touch with their families and friends in ways that were once unimaginable. Deployed service members now have access to the Internet and e-mail, cellular telephones, satellite telephones, and efficient surface and airmail services. However, these conveniences should be used with care and common sense. Easy access to instant communication can create new problems, making it more difficult for you and your loved ones to cope with separation. For example, when we feel we have the luxury of time and access, we tend to spend more time sharing information about negative experiences, aggravations, fears, and problems. As a result, loved ones may suffer a great deal more stress and concern than they might otherwise.

Communicate wisely. Be honest and trustworthy, but try to balance your sharing of positive and negative information. Try to remember that those who love you will also worry about you, and they may already feel frustrated by a sense of helplessness. If possible, discuss problems they might be able to help you solve by actions they can take at home on your behalf. In general, people suffer less stress when they believe they can do something to improve a bad situation.

Communicate effectively. Talk about your feelings constructively to reduce your own sense of isolation. Acknowledge that it is helpful to share emotional information with your loved ones. Ask about what's going on at home only to the extent that you really want to know. If you feel frustrated by helplessness, say so and ask for patience and understanding.

Communicate with empathy. Empathy is a term psychologists use to describe our capacity to appreciate others' feelings and feel for them. When we are physically separated from others, we have to work much harder to describe our own experiences and understand the experiences of others. Try to remember that this may be frustrating for all concerned and look for ways to connect as deeply as possible in spite of frustration. The positive outcome of empathy is that it provides comfort and assurance, both of which can be given and received even in the absence of full knowledge or understanding. Seek and accept this reassurance from loved ones. The benefits will be obvious, both during and after your deployment.

LIVING AND DELIVERING IN COMBAT

Serving in combat can be stressful even though it is also empowering, exhilarating, and exciting. Many soldiers look back at their combat service as a profoundly positive experience that helped them grow and become more confident and effective in their lives and in their work. Although the risks you face in combat can never be fully controlled, you can control our own outlook, expectations, reactions, and behavior. By learning what to expect and how to respond, you can perform more effectively and get the most out of your combat experience.

A squad leader looks back for a casualty evacuation helicopter in the middle of a six-hour firefight with Taliban insurgents. *U.S. Marine Corps/1st Lt Kurt Stahl*

Under combat conditions, you must know how to control your mental focus and ensure that your attention is where it needs to be. We all inhabit two different worlds: the world outside us, and our own inner (psychological, intellectual) world. When you are involved in combat operations, your attention should be focused primarily on the world around you. Your mind should be directed to where you are and what you must do. When we are threatened, we naturally direct our focus outward to identify the source of the threat and respond appropriately. In combat, you must learn to maintain an appropriately high level of arousal and alertness in constant anticipation of threat. Instead of letting your mind relax its attention to your inner world, you must keep your focus outward to the world in which a threat may present itself at any time and a fast response may be necessary. You will have time later, when you are safe, to consider and analyze your experience.

Outward focus is also helpful as a strategy to avoid the distraction of fear, anger, frustration, and other emotions that might interfere with effective performance in combat. In fact, nature has equipped you with an automatic tendency to focus outward when you are injured. In response to injury, the brain turns off pain signals for a short time. This provides a "grace period" as an opportunity to respond as needed without the distraction of pain.

People who encounter dangerous situations on a regular basis can learn to manage their natural responses in a positive and effective way. Dangerous situations produce real physical and mental changes that we cannot turn off at will. The goal here is not to suppress but to master. It is possible to turn the body's physical and psychological responses to one's own advantage and benefit. Many soldiers report an immense sense of empowerment and satisfaction in learning to master their mental and physical responses in combat.

RESILIENCE IN COMBAT

In Chapter 3 of this book, we introduced the subject of psychological resilience to stress. Resilience is a common capacity that has much to do with an optimistic outlook, orientation to challenge, realistic expectations, and a sense of dedication to purpose. Although resilience can be viewed as a source of strength, it is important to understand that psychological injury is not the result of weakness. Mental strength can be seen much the same as physical strength. Just as physical injury can be inflicted upon strong bodies, psychological injury can be inflicted upon strong minds. When you train your body to improve your physi-

A team leader shouts an order to one of his Marines before beginning a patrol in Fallujah, Iraq.
U.S. Marine Corps/Lance Cpl. Christopher J. Zahn

cal strength and fitness, your real goal is to improve your performance. Although good performance does not guarantee you will never be injured, it reduces the likelihood of some injuries and enhances your overall survivability. Likewise, there are things you can do to promote psychological survival by improving your overall psychological performance in combat.

The key features of resilience are typical among members of the military service, who are usually highly motivated to serve in combat. So it is not surprising that most combat veterans thrive and take a positive view of their experience in combat, often describing it as exciting, satisfying, rewarding, and meaningful. More often than not, combat experience has a positive overall impact on the lives of those who serve.

U.S. Army soldiers patrol an area near the village of Kowtay, Khowst province, Afghanistan. *Photo courtesy of the U.S. Army/Staff Sgt Andrew Smith*

Combat service is sometimes described as life on the edge, where the edge is an inherently dangerous but exciting place. The skills you acquire in combat can help you later in life in other settings. Your resulting confidence, skill, and perspective can be put to use as self-discipline and improved performance on and off the battlefield, in or out of uniform. Research now suggests that although the stress of combat may be difficult, it can also make soldiers better and stronger persons in their daily lives. Through your experiences in combat, you can gain a renewed appreciation for life, enhanced personal strength, increased tolerance for stress, and a broader view of life's possibilities and your own abilities. Even those who experience very negative and long-lasting reactions to stress or trauma can also experience the benefits of what some researchers describe as post-traumatic growth.

SPECIAL CONSIDERATIONS FOR RESERVISTS AND
NATIONAL GUARD MEMBERS

Historically, our military reserve forces have not been expected to deploy as often as active duty military personnel. During long periods of stability such as the Cold War, reservists were rarely deployed. Many reservists were deployed during the Gulf War but then experienced several years without the imminent prospect of deployment. In recent years, however, U.S. military reservists have been deployed repeatedly, with comparatively little time at home between deployments. These new demands and expectations have been unusually difficult for reservists and their families.

Although the active and reserve components of our armed forces are more alike than different, reservists do confront some unique challenges and concerns. These are most obvious when the reservist is faced with orders to deploy. For the reservist, deployment introduces a host of special concerns and unique problems, such as the possibility of job loss, uncertain family support resources, and doubts about readiness.

YOUR JOB

If you are a reservist, your military service is probably not your primary source of income. You probably rely more heavily upon one or more other sources of full-time employment in the civilian sector. This is as important as an economic reality as it is a matter of your individual identity and the role you play within your family and your community. It is reasonable to be concerned about the im-

Air Force reservists complete maintenance checklists onboard a C-17 prior to takeoff. *U.S. Air Force photo/Capt. Marnee A.C. Losurdo*

Marine reservists during a seven-month tour of duty in the Northern Fallujah and Saqlawiyah areas of Iraq. *U.S. Marine Corps/Cpl Mike Escobar*

pact of deployment on your civilian employment status and long-term economic security. It is also reasonable to consider the potential difficulty of resuming your role as a civilian after deployment.

The potential economic impact of deployment depends upon what sort of civilian work you performed prior to deployment. If you have been employed outside the home, there are laws in place to protect you from job loss. The Uniformed Services Employment and Reemployment Rights Act (USERRA) of 1994 was enacted to encourage Guard and Reserve service and prohibit job discrimination against those who serve. More information about the law and your rights can be found at the Employer Support of the Guard and Reserve website (http://esgr.org), which also offers links to a variety of other services, forms, and training opportunities. The Veterans Employment Opportunities Act also provides veterans with preferred access to federal job opportunities. Additional information about federal preferences and job opportunities can be found through the U.S. Department of Labor (www.dol.gov/vets/programs/vetspref/main.htm) and the Office of Personnel Management (http://www.opm.gov/veterans/html/vetsinfo.asp).

Unfortunately, not all employers respect job protection laws as they should. Even if you are not concerned with the possibility that you might lose your job, you might have reasonable worries about the impact of prolonged absence on your job skills, training, professional competitiveness, and future promotions.

You may find yourself struggling to catch up with your non-military employment commitments when you return. You may find that less experienced workers have advanced in your absence. Depending on your position and employment circumstance, it might be helpful to talk with your employer and request guidance in advance.

If you are self-employed or own your own business, you may be understandably concerned about how your business might suffer while you are gone. In this case, you may want to consider hiring someone to take your place temporarily. Reservists who do not work outside the home sometimes incur an additional financial burden to provide replacement caretakers for home and/or family members. Consider asking if family members and friends would be able and willing to accept and share this workload.

Whatever your work situation may be, you should recognize that deployment preparation itself can demand a good deal of time and attention. For example, your employer may ask that you help to inform, prepare, and train coworkers to perform specific duties in your absence. These additional demands will come even as you work harder at home to prepare family members and friends to manage well in your absence. At times, it may seem as though preparation for deployment is a job in its own right.

YOUR FAMILY

Psychologists know that we are better able to prepare psychologically for stressful or life-changing events when we can predict their occurrence. When deployment is unpredictable, it is more difficult to adjust, prepare, reduce, or control the effects of stress. Uncertainty makes the situation more difficult for the reservist and for his or her immediate and extended family members, friends, coworkers, and community members.

In the face of uncertainty, it can be very helpful to focus on matters within your control. For example, you can take the initiative to identify family support services and resources before you receive deployment notice. This is an area of particular concern for reservists and their families, whose needs are unique and may be less predictable or certain than that of active duty members. For ex-

Army reservists check map coordinates during the Army Reserves' Best Warrior Competition held at Fort Knox. *Photo courtesy of the U.S. Army/Staff Sgt Jeremy Rondone*

ample, the civilian spouses and children of military reservists may have few or no friends who share or understand their experience. Because some reserve units are located far from major military installations and facilities, key counseling and support services may be difficult to access. The armed services have been generally proactive in trying to extend support to reservists and their families, but it can be difficult to serve personnel who are scattered over large geographic areas. By identifying and contacting support services in advance, you can better prepare yourself and your family to meet specific needs that could arise in the future. If months or years have passed since previous access, you may find that policies, programs, personnel, and facilities have changed. You can reduce the stress by familiarizing yourself with current procedures and programs before the need becomes urgent.

Because reserve unit social support networks are sometimes not as strong, organized, or richly interconnected as social networks typical of active service military units, it can be more difficult for reservists' families to maintain communication with their deployed members. To make things yet more complicated, reservists are sometimes cross leveled into entirely new, more distant units before they deploy. Here again, it may be helpful to consider these issues well before deployment becomes a reality. Through discussions with family members, coworkers, fellow soldiers, and military leaders, you can try to identify creative strategies and solutions to increase and sustain communication with loved ones during periods of deployment. This will help to reduce the stress of uncertainty.

YOUR READINESS

When you are deployed for the first time or after a long period at home, it is understandable if you experience doubts about your readiness to perform as a full-time soldier. Unit members depend upon each other to perform their jobs well. In combat, your proficiency can literally make the difference between life and death for you and for your fellow warfighters. If you are unsure about your readiness to perform, make an effort to talk with others who have recently returned from deployment. There are now many forums, official and informal, through which soldiers share their combat experiences and insights. Read books, talk to people, and be proactive to ensure your readiness.

The stresses of modern military life are real and substantial, especially in times of war. As a reservist, you may have had less experience than active duty personnel in coping with the demands of military service. As a result, you may need additional time to build psychological resilience to the stress of full-time duty. This is a common challenge among reservists, who are often affected differently by the stresses of full-time deployment than their active service counterparts. Rates of some service-related health issues (e.g., Gulf War Syndrome and post-traumatic stress disorder) typically differ between active and reserve components. Although risk factors such as age may help explain some differences, it is also likely that when reservists are deployed for the first time, they are at least initially somewhat more susceptible to stress and its possible negative effects on overall health. Being aware of this puts you in a better position to understand your concerns and experiences and to seek help and support when needed.

CULTURE, COHESION, AND COMMUNITY

Elsewhere in this volume you will find a discussion of some of the issues involved in adapting to and working in different cultures. While the differences between American culture and the culture of an Arab Islamic nation are apparent, there are other cultural differences that are far more subtle but nevertheless very real and as deserving of your thought and attention. For example, there are cultural differences among different kinds of units, between the different branches of service, and between the active and reserve components of the U.S. military.

Psychologists know that a natural part of human social interaction is to identify as a part of a larger social group. The military, with its emphasis on unit identification and explicit hierarchical relationships, encourages this kind of identification because it builds cohesion and morale, commits unit members to a common purpose, and establishes an accepted set of norms for social interaction, job expectations, and the like. These are all positive consequences, but there can be negative consequences as well.

Negative consequences can arise when we begin to behave differently toward people exclusively or mainly on the basis of the group to which they belong. Sometimes awareness of cultural differences in the military is expressed in terms of good-natured banter, for example when ground soldiers talk about how much more luxurious life is on an air base. Other times, excessive focus on what is different between units, branches, or components can obscure the more important things they share in common. While it is true that active and reserve component soldiers may serve in different ways, sometimes facing different challenges, it is more important to recognize that all service members are American warfighters who sacrifice much for the common good.

LEADERSHIP, UNIT COHESION, AND MORALE

Military operations can demand as much of you psychologically as they do physically. Well-led, highly motivated, and well-disciplined troops can defeat larger, better-equipped, but poorly motivated forces. Strong morale and unit cohesion are essential to military success. At the core of an effective military force are leaders who can inspire, motivate, and sustain the morale of others.

FORMAL AND INFORMAL LEADERSHIP

Officers and NCOs hold formal authority and are expected to exercise effective leadership. However, you can also exercise informal leadership within your unit. You can help motivate other unit members by direct encouragement, by creative initiative, and by example. You can strengthen your unit's sense of purpose and dedication to mission success by demonstrating determined performance under pressure.

Peer influence is a powerful motivator. By helping your fellow soldiers develop the skills they will need to handle their assigned duties, you improve their confidence and effectiveness. Perhaps just as important, your supportive efforts will show that you are someone who can be counted upon to help others when needed. Confidence in self and others can bolster courage and action when it is needed in combat.

You can also exercise informal leadership by providing officers and NCOs with helpful feedback and suggestions concerning new or changing priorities and problems, resource allocation, and innovative ways to accomplish mission objectives. Of course, you should never challenge the authority of your formal leadership. Rather, make it clear that you are trying to support his or her efforts to ensure mission success. Good leaders recognize and appreciate the value of helpful support, new information, and creative initiative. Look for opportunities to exercise informal leadership among your peers and assist your formal leadership in ways that promote mission success. By learning and exercising informal leadership, you can develop skills that are critical to success and survival in military life and service. These include innovative thinking, adaptability, organization, initiative, and problem solving, all of which are essential to fighting and winning on the modern battlefield.

Effective military leaders know how to motivate and harness the full potential of their troops' talents and skills. Good leadership creates a climate that empowers soldiers to lead one another through challenge and hardship. Officers and NCOs can motivate soldiers to become informal leaders by treating them as valued contributing members of the team, encouraging them to take initiatives, and actively seeking their ideas and suggestions. Officers and NCOs who view and treat their subordinates as sources of informal leadership will inspire soldiers to think and behave accordingly. Certainly, individuals will vary in the degree to which they are willing and able to exercise informal leadership. The important thing is to let them know they have the capacity and freedom do so. When subordinates view themselves as active contributors to mission success, they are more likely to apply the full extent of their skills and capabilities. This, in turn, promotes additional motivation, development, growth, and unit morale.

At all levels of command, leadership requires competence and trust. Consider your circumstances now and in the past and recall that your willingness and enthusiasm to follow orders has always been influenced by your faith in the competence of your leaders. As a direct result of your faith in their competence and your knowledge of their commitment, you trusted your leaders—you were willing to rely upon their judgment in the belief that they acted in the best interest of all concerned. Trust may take time to develop and is often put to the test by new challenges and difficulties.

Competence and trust are not endpoints but rather ongoing processes that require dedication to self-improvement and working with others. Commitment to these processes also plays an essential role in building and sustaining unit cohesion and morale. In the absence of trust among members of a military unit, unit cohesion breaks down and morale quickly begins to suffer. In the absence of trust between soldiers and their leaders, leadership is weakened and missions may fail. Leaders who lose the trust of their subordinates typically resort to authoritarian, punitive styles of command. These strategies further erode unit cohesion and morale.

CONCLUSION

Military leaders are sometimes accused of focusing too much on the past and not adequately preparing for future demands. Given the pace of change in modern society, it is not surprising that anyone should find it difficult to anticipate major geopolitical events such as the fall of the Soviet Union or the attacks of September 11, 2001. In the midst of change, American warfighters have always been known for their adaptability, their commitment to country, and comradeship, no matter what the challenge. This is the foundation upon which American military success is built.

As a member of the U.S. armed forces, you represent all of these same characteristics on an individual level. You are adaptable, dedicated, and professional. Your knowledge and experience is gained in service to something greater than yourself. Whatever the challenge, you can meet it with confidence and a sense of place and purpose founded in the best of military tradition.

While it would be comforting to pretend that we know what the future holds, the fact is that we do not and cannot predict the future. We may or may not face another war such as those fought in Iraq and Afghanistan. Future wars may involve primarily naval forces and airpower—but can we be sure of this? By thinking realistically about what it means to be a member of the U.S. armed services in the twenty-first century, you can better prepare for the challenges and uncertainties of modern military service. We cannot predict the future, but we—and you—can prepare and be ready to respond as effectively as possible.

CHAPTER FIVE

From Combat to Home

Most combat veterans feel an immense sense of pride and honor for having served their country with dignity and courage. They also know that combat is a life-changing experience. Years later, combat veterans may still struggle with feelings of fear, anger, or frustration when they recall frightening moments or gruesome images. For others, ironically, the stress of combat may be overshadowed by the stress of coming home.

During long periods of deployment, you and your family will live very different lives under very different conditions. It is paradoxical that while you miss each other most, you will also discover by necessity that you can function effectively while living apart from one another. At times, you may find it difficult to understand or appreciate the concerns and priorities of those at home. When you finally return to the daily concerns of civilian life, readjustment may be more difficult than you expect. Weeks or months after returning from deployment, you may feel a lingering sense of detachment and distance from the life you once took for granted as ordinary. The possibility of redeployment can make this sense of distance seem inescapable and permanent.

The purpose of this chapter is to consider the most important adjustments and challenges you may face when you return home from combat. In particular, it is important for you to know what to expect, how to stay safe, and how to rebuild important relationships. Finally, we look ahead to preparing for life after the military.

Soldiers wait in line to board an Air Force C-17 that will take them back to the United States from Joint Base Balad, Iraq. *U.S. Air Force photo/Tech. Sgt. Erik Gudmundson*

THE NEW NORMAL

Returning home to a happy reunion with loved ones is an event that is much anticipated by soldiers, their families, and their friends. However, it is important to understand in advance that the initial thrill of reunion is often followed by significant challenges and difficulties. Just as deployment can be a demanding and transformational experience for the soldier, coping with its effects at home may also be a demanding and transformational experience for family members and friends. The comforts of home—and those who live there—may not be exactly as you remember them. By anticipating and preparing for change, you can ease your transition back into family and community life. The costs and benefits of military service will stay with you throughout your life.

When you return home from combat, you bring with you—in your mind, heart, and body—all of your combat experiences. Some were good experiences. Some were bad. How they affect you in the long run will depend to a large extent on how you choose to think about them and how you make sense of them in the context of your previously "normal" life. When you face new challenges associated with coming home, consider that your efforts to adjust and cope with

Soldiers returning home from Iraq and Afghanistan are greeted by friends and family. *National Guard*

difficulties can be seen as an extension and continuation of your service and sacrifice. Adjustment to change requires courage, commitment, and hard work. This process will take time, and it may take some effort on your part. In your absence, your family members also had new experiences. They, too, will need time to adjust.

When you first arrive back home after combat, you might initially feel elated by the opportunity to do lots of little things you have missed. After many months spent living in a war zone, the simple comforts of home can feel like great luxuries. At first, shopping for groceries or doing laundry might seem like great fun. But, of course, you know this is temporary. You might even want this fun phase to pass more quickly because you want things to feel fully normal again. Even as you enjoy the thrill of returning home to a civilian environment, you may experience an odd sense of disconnection, as if you're watching your life as a movie rather than living it. You may be distracted by thoughts of unfinished business left behind in war or by intrusive memories of experiences you meant to leave behind. The daily activities of home life might seem superficial or trivial by comparison. And you may wonder how you'll ever bridge the gap between yourself—a changed person, now a veteran of combat—and those you love, whose experiences have been quite different.

Post-deployment return to garrison always involves a period of reintegration. There is paperwork to be done and briefings to be attended. There may be high expectations about block leave, when your entire unit enjoys an extended period of time off. Extended leave does provide an opportunity to begin easing back into the regular duties of home life. However, you should not expect that a few weeks of leave is all you will need to complete your transition. Often, leave time is necessary just to discover that you will need more time to fully readjust. During your post-deployment leave, you will probably realize that transition isn't only about readjusting to once familiar daily chores, routines, and schedules. More significant transitions will be necessary in many areas of your life, including all aspects of your relationships with family members.

PSYCHOLOGICAL AND EMOTIONAL REACTIONS

Each individual has his or her own way of responding to post-deployment transition. Most people experience some amount of stress when they return home after combat. Some find it difficult to adjust, while others do not. For some, post-deployment readjustment is an extremely stressful and difficult process.

No matter how you feel about transition, it is important to remember that you are not the only person to have endured this experience. Your feelings are not unusual or wrong. If you find the experience difficult, it may be useful to consider that readjustment involves your mind as well as your body. After prolonged exposure to combat-related stress, your body may also need time to rediscover its former state of normal biochemical and hormonal balance.

WITHDRAWAL AND DEPRESSION

The complicated process of psychological and physical healing can produce symptoms such as withdrawal and depression, anxiety, sleep disturbance, numbness, anger, hypervigilance, nervousness, jumpiness, guilt, and irritability. These reactions are usually temporary, can be managed individually or with help, and should resolve gradually over the course of one to three months. If symptoms of depression, anger, or sleep problems persist for more than two months, you should seek help from a health care professional. There is obvious cause for concern if, after a few weeks at home, you feel worse instead of better, are

Going out with the inten- tion of only drinking a small amount and ending up drunk, or altering one's life- style and habits to incorpo- rate drinking, are signs of an emerging dependence on alcohol. *U.S. Marine Corps/ Lance Cpl. James W. Clark*

using alcohol or drugs to cope, or find yourself engaging in risky, undisciplined, or unlawful behavior.

Some combat veterans experience depression related to feelings of guilt for actions taken during deployment or being unable to relate effectively to fam- ily members. Guilt usually manifests as self-blame or repeated second-guessing about what has happened and why. The individual who suffers from a persistent sense of guilt may feel that he or she does not deserve to enjoy living. Over time, persons plagued by guilt may feel paralyzed, unable to solve problems or move forward. If you experience such thoughts and feelings, it is best that you consult with a chaplain, mental health professional, or trusted friend who can help you put difficult experiences in fair perspective.

ANGER

Anger is not an inherently bad emotion. What matters is how you choose to be- have when you feel angry. Anger can be used productively if you see it as a signal that something is wrong and let it inspire you to correct the situation.

Unfortunately, anger more often provokes negative or harmful behavior. When we are angry, we sometimes say or do things we later regret. Anger in- terferes with good judgment and decision-making. Angry behavior often has serious and destructive consequences.

Anger management isn't so much about managing anger itself as it is about managing the behavior that can result from it. Self-control is an important skill for service members to practice under the best of circumstances. It is absolutely essential that you exert rational control over your behavior when you experience feelings of anger and aggression. This might be easily overlooked after months of living in a combat environment, where split-second aggressive behavior may have been essential to survival. By contrast, in garrison and at home, your health and survival—and that of others—will depend on your ability to behave rationally, without violence or aggression.

Be aware that when you first come home, you may have a short fuse. Consider safe, healthy ways to cope with frustration, anger, and irritability. Get regular exercise. Avoid alcohol. Take time—perhaps lots of time—between feeling anger and taking action. Try to find the humor in difficult situations and in your own reactions to them. Above all, try to keep some sense of perspective about what matters and what does not matter. Talk with close friends who can provide a reality check. Never reach for your weapon in anger. If you feel you are on the verge of losing control or threatening the safety of others, seek help. If people comment that you seem to be having problems managing your anger, take them seriously and find help.

WHEN ANGER IS OUT OF CONTROL . . .

✓ You are irritable or impatient most of the time.
✓ You have frequent disagreements with friends, family, and coworkers.
✓ You lose your temper (yelling, slamming doors, etc.).
✓ You fantasize or threaten violence against your spouse, girlfriend, children, or others.
✓ Friends or family members encourage you to get help, telling you that you have a problem with anger.

SIGNS AND SYMPTOMS OF HYPERVIGILANCE

✓ Nervous tension, anxiety
✓ Easily startled, jumpy
✓ Fear response to loud noises
✓ Sleep disturbance
✓ Nightmares and/or flashbacks
✓ Poor concentration

HYPERVIGILANCE

Hypervigilance is a form of anxiety that can develop in response to stress or trauma. It is rather like being in a persistent state of fight-or-flight response. Without relief, it can be exhausting.

Hypervigilance can also be a symptom of more extensive difficulties such as combat stress reaction, now better known as post-traumatic stress disorder (PTSD). It is important to understand that an individual might have a few symptoms of hypervigilance (for example, flashbacks, nightmares, startled reactions) and not necessarily be suffering from PTSD. PTSD-like symptoms can be the result of other problems such as depression, anger, extreme anxiety, or sleep deprivation. Without a full and careful analysis of individual history and symptoms, PTSD may be difficult to diagnose. If you are concerned that early symptoms of post-deployment hypervigilance might be getting worse, or if your symptoms interfere with your ability to concentrate and function effectively in your daily life, you should request guidance from a health care professional.

INDISCIPLINE AND RISKY BEHAVIOR

Behavior can be a powerful indicator of emotional status. Sometimes, we suspect that a friend or coworker might be suffering because we observe obvious changes in his or her behavior. If a fellow soldier returns from deployment and begins to behave in ways that are uncharacteristically careless, sloppy, undisciplined, unlawful, or dangerous, it is reasonable to conclude that he or she may require help. Early signs of trouble might include self-defeating behavior such as lack of discipline, persistent lateness, multiple missed deadlines, or insubordination. If these behavioral issues are overlooked or ignored, they may grow worse instead of better.

Some individuals find it very difficult to readjust to the relatively benign, sometimes boring routines of daily life. Although combat may be chaotic, stressful, and frightening, it is never boring. It may be difficult for some individuals to transition away from the constant adrenaline rush of life in a war zone. Once home, they may begin to engage in risky or dangerous behavior that provides a similar sense of danger. The problem, of course, is that dangerous behavior is dangerous—it presents a risk to self and others. If you know of someone who appears to be engaged in reckless or dangerous behavior, do

RISKY BEHAVIOR
✓ Carrying a loaded weapon; keeping loaded weapon in the car
✓ Failing to practice weapon safety; keeping unsecured weapons at home
Dangerous Driving
✓ Speeding, reckless driving, racing
✓ Driving under the influence of alcohol or other drugs
Substance Abuse
✓ Using alcohol to sleep
✓ Drinking to get drunk or forget
✓ Buying, selling, or using illegal drugs
✓ Using drugs prescribed for other people or purposes
Antisocial Behavior
✓ Fighting
✓ Stealing
✓ Vandalism
✓ Violence against people or animals

not remain silent. If you feel comfortable talking to the individual directly about the problem, do so. If not, then seek advice or assistance from a trusted source, such as another member of your unit, a unit leader, a medical or mental health professional, or a chaplain.

Grief

For many combat veterans, the most difficult lingering effect of war is grief. Some people deal with grief openly, while others deal with it more privately. If you have dealt with loss before, you may be better prepared for the experience. But you should also be aware that the losses of war can be uniquely difficult to accept. Death in war is usually violent, and those who die are young. Soldiers are killed suddenly, and sometimes arbitrarily. When people die by sudden violence, those left behind often struggle with the need to believe that violence is controllable and death is preventable. When close friends are wounded or killed in battle, grief may be combined with feelings of guilt for having survived or having not been present at the time. Fellow soldiers may wonder if they did enough to save their buddies. They may blame themselves or others for decisions or actions that led to the loss.

Grief cannot be rushed or fixed. It may come in waves. It may be triggered by certain types of events (anniversaries, holidays), memories (shared experiences), or reminders (songs, photographs). It takes time to accept loss and recognize that death is sometimes senseless and unpreventable. It

ALCOHOL: ASSESSING AND MANAGING YOUR PERSONAL RISK

Many service members feel a need to catch up on drinking alcohol when they return home from deployment. An occasional drink is not a bad thing, but too much can be dangerous.

To prevent alcohol-related accidents, incidents, and negative health consequences, it is important to limit consumption. It is also important to consider one's own motivations. Problems arise when people drink in an effort to get drunk, forget problems, relieve depression, vent anger, cope, or sleep. If you use alcohol in an effort to solve or ignore emotional or psychological pain, you will find that this strategy does not work. When treated with alcohol, such problems grow worse instead of better.

These are classic warning signs of alcohol abuse or dependency:

✓ You notice that you are drinking more than you used to (e.g., pre-deployment).
✓ You have thoughts that maybe you should cut back or stop drinking, but you don't follow through.
✓ Other people make comments or express concern about your drinking behavior.
✓ You feel the need for a drink when you wake up in the morning.
✓ You take risks, such as driving under the influence of alcohol or riding as a passenger with a driver who has been drinking.

If any of these signs apply to you, seek professional help as soon as possible, before the drinking problem gets out of control.

takes time to forgive oneself or to forgive others for failing to have foreseen or prevented the unimaginable. Sadness may never subside entirely. Over time, however, feelings of sadness will be less intense and less painful.

Perhaps the greatest challenge associated with grief and loss is giving oneself permission to get on with life. If you experience grief, it is important to keep tabs on your own psychological well-being. Do you feel unable to enjoy life? Do you feel undeserving of joy? Are you burdened by guilt? Are you constantly distracted by second-guessing events that led up to the loss?

Do you use drugs or alcohol to cope with your grief? Do you suffer from nightmares or intrusive memories? If you answer yes to any of these, or if the intensity of your pain does not change over time, you should talk to someone you trust, such as a chaplain or mental health professional.

In coping with grief, it is sometimes helpful to say goodbye by participating in memorial services or other ceremonies, laying a wreath at a grave site, communicating with your friend's family members, or sharing your thoughts and memories in writing. If you can do any or all of these things in a personally meaningful way, it may help you find peace and move on.

STIGMA

When psychological and emotional effects of war don't improve on their own, you should turn to a chaplain or mental health professional for help. However, studies have shown that individuals who most need help are often least likely to seek it. Often, service members fail to seek help because they fear they may be seen as weak or impaired. They are concerned that they may be embarrassed or ridiculed, their personal information might not be kept confidential, or their careers might suffer if people find out they are receiving mental health care services. Of course, these concerns are not unique to the military; many civilians express similar concerns. The irony here is that individuals demonstrate great courage when they recognize the need for help. The decision to seek help is a sign of strength, commitment, and self-awareness.

Although stigma certainly persists in some settings and units, more and more people have come to understand that mental health care is an essential part of overall health care. The U.S. military also recognizes the importance of mental health care and has made a significant investment in supporting it. In garrison and on deployment, mental health care is now considered to play a key role in overall readiness. Military leaders and organizational policies set an increasingly positive tone for this effort and are encouraged to respect confidentiality and provide time and privacy as necessary for appointments during duty hours.

You can make an important contribution to improving the climate that surrounds mental health care. Consider the importance of good mental health and respect those who seek help when needed. Do not joke or gossip about those who need support from mental health care providers. If you see that a friend or coworker is having problems, offer to help that person locate resources or services as needed. Consider that people's lives and experiences may be more complicated than you know. Remember that your own life might one day depend on another person's healthy adjustment.

Readjustment and Relationships at Work

Some service members find it difficult to transition from the high-stakes work they performed in combat to the more mundane and less dangerous work they are tasked to do in garrison, perhaps in an entirely new unit. After carrying a high level of responsibility in combat, noncombat duty might seem boring by comparison. The difference between combat and noncombat work is real and dramatic. As a result, some combat veterans struggle with low motivation, boredom, disappointment, anger, and insubordination. One helpful strategy is to talk about life and work in combat with those who haven't yet experienced it. It may also be helpful to focus on preparing for your next deployment.

Combat veterans might also have trouble adapting to new leadership, especially if a new leader is seen as inexperienced. Some soldiers report that they find it difficult to take seriously the orders and efforts of a new leader who has not experienced combat. In this situation, you must rely upon your basic military discipline and understand that new leaders might appreciate the opportunity to learn from your experience. The same holds true for integrating new personnel into your unit. At first, it may seem difficult to relate to someone who did not share your experience in combat. By talking about your experience, you can give the new person an opportunity to learn and benefit by your experience. He or she will probably appreciate this as an opportunity to connect with the unit. At some point, you could also find yourself in a new unit and feel disconnected or lonely because no one understands where you have been, what you have done, and what you have endured. Remember that these feelings are normal and it can take time to feel comfortable with a new unit. It may be helpful to stay in touch with friends from your previous unit.

RELATIONSHIPS AT HOME

Combat veterans often return from war with a renewed positive perspective on life and the importance of their relationships with family and friends. This provides a strong basis for transition, supported by a commitment to make the most out of life. Where there is a desire to hang on to this new sense of purpose, there is strength to work through the confusion and stress that sometimes occurs through the process of readjustment.

One way to improve your own transition is to talk with those who are close to you about the experiences you have had and how they may have changed you. It may be difficult at first to tell your story. It may seem impossible to explain it to someone who wasn't there. You must try anyway and accept that while it may not be possible to explain every detail or context, it is important to share what knowledge you can with loved ones. Take some time to think about what you wish to share and why. In order to understand your new reality and reactions to it, people who are close to you need to know something about your experience. Sometimes we gain new insight by telling our stories aloud. By telling your story, you create an opportunity to reconnect with loved ones, give them a chance to understand something about life in combat, and open the door to additional perspective.

You have no obligation to share your experience with people who aren't close to you, but this might not stop them from asking questions. Questions from strangers can be silly and irritating. The most common questions are, "Did you kill someone?" and "What was it like?" Though such questions may be aggravating, remember that people are understandably curious and interested. Most people don't know how silly their questions might sound to you. Rather than feel annoyed, remember that you can decide how to handle yourself in response. Decide in advance how you wish to answer various questions so you won't feel you've been put on the spot when people ask. It might be best to keep your answer brief and to the point to discourage additional questions.

Meanwhile, some combat veterans are surprised when people do not ask questions. This might mean that people are trying to be respectful. They might care very much and wish to learn more but not want to intrude or impose. In this case, it might help if you introduce the subject to let them know when you are ready to talk.

You and Your Spouse

Very few occupations demand the high level of family commitment that is required by military service. Military personnel and their spouses must be able to tolerate a high level of uncertainty about their lives together and apart. It is essentially true that if a marriage is strong going into a deployment, it will remain strong coming out of deployment. But what does it mean to have a strong marriage? It may not mean the same thing for every married couple.

Generally, couples who weather the demands of deployment describe the partner at home as independent, able to work within the system, and supportive of his or her service member's commitment to serve. These same couples usually describe the military partner as patient, flexible, and tolerant of shifts in decision-making power. If these characteristics describe the makings of a successful marriage, it is also important to recognize that even the most successful relationships can be challenged by the practical realities of deployment. Individuals who are married to military personnel are generally proud of their accomplishments and sacrifice. And yet in the loneliness of separation, a spouse left at home may endure periods of anxiety, depression, resentment, and anger.

Just as military planners know what to expect throughout the various stages of the deployment cycle, it may help military couples to prepare for different phases of emotional adjustment such as anticipation (pre-deployment), emotional withdrawal (deployment), and excitement (post-deployment).

During the exciting period just prior to a service member's return home, spouses on both sides of the deployment line are showered with reintegration briefings, preparatory brochures, and informational websites. This information may be very helpful indeed. But when the excitement subsides, there remains the challenge of learning to live together again as a couple. You may wonder how to regain your unique sense of closeness with your spouse and how to reestablish or redefine new and former roles and responsibilities.

Most couples have great expectations of reunion and getting close again. They may enjoy a honeymoon period that lasts for a few days. But after the initial joy of reunion, many couples experience disappointment or conflict. Normal reactions may include emotional highs and lows, irritability, and crying episodes. These reactions sometimes continue for a month or two. Remember that it takes time to reestablish emotional intimacy. Communication is essential. Service members who have had this experience report that the best strategy is to take it slow and make time for one another. Understand that each partner needs his or her own time to readjust. Among other things, you and your spouse may need time to confront and accept the difference between idealistic expectations and strenuous realities. This struggle may apply to emotional intimacy as well as sexual intimacy. In each case, the best approach is to communicate, be patient, and maintain a sense of perspective and humor.

One important aspect of intimacy is the ability to work together and see yourself and your spouse as a team. In this case, it is especially important to consider how your deployment experience may have changed the way you behave or interact with others when you are trying to accomplish a goal. Your spouse may perceive you to be more difficult to work with if you are experiencing readjustment reactions such as irritability or anxiety. It is important that you be willing to listen and discuss these reactions. Reassure yourself and your spouse that you are aware of your reactions and that they are normal and probably temporary. If you still have trouble working with your spouse after two months or so, it may be a good idea to seek his or her support to find assistance from others. Taking care of yourself is critical to taking care of your family.

Even as deployment may leave you with a heightened sense of appreciation for life, this can leave you feeling somewhat impatient with daily tasks and responsibilities that strike you as mundane or trivial. There is a need to find balance between your perspective on the big picture and the practical needs of ordinary life. Understand that your spouse may have looked forward to once again sharing the load. For him or her, ordinary chores may take on extraordinary significance as evidence of your safe return and continued commitment. However you and your partner regard life's daily chores, someone will have to do them. It is important to do your share and to recognize that apparently trivial chores are actually very important to maintaining a safe, happy, and healthy household.

Who does what? During your deployment, the spouse you leave behind will have to assume responsibility for all major and minor household tasks and decisions. Some spouses are more than happy to readjust when the service member returns from deployment. Others may find it difficult to give over or share responsibility. In either case, it is probably a mistake to expect that you can return home and pick up exactly where you left off. The reality of military family life is that couples must be flexible, but this is sometimes easier said than done. When an individual has gained mastery over a new task, it may be difficult to relinquish responsibility and trust someone else to do the job as well. During prolonged deployment, the little tasks of life may assume symbolic value as great achievements or aggravating resentments. Be prepared that it may take time to reintegrate. Newly stable routines cannot be established or reestablished overnight. Remember that your spouse's independence was essential to your success while you were away. Value and acknowledge the importance of your spouse's hard work and success. Remember too that what works for other couples may not work for you.

During post-deployment transition, missteps are inevitable. On any given day, one or both partners may feel rejected or overburdened. Each may feel the need to express frustration, disappointment, or resentment that built up during separation. Once again, it is important to be open and honest about these experiences. Good communication is critical to recognizing and managing shifts in decision-making and control.

Finally, you may return home to find that your spouse has found new interests, activities, hobbies, and friends. If these changes seem hard to understand or accept, remember that they represent the intelligent coping and survival of an independent spouse whose commitment and energy is essential to a successful military marriage. Consider that it may be unreasonable to expect to come home and find nothing different in his or her life. If you find yourself feeling confused or resentful of changes in your spouse, be honest about this while accepting that your own expectations may not have been fair.

YOU AND YOUR CHILDREN

For service members with children, the reintegration process is an especially bittersweet time. The joy of seeing children after a long separation is intense, but the sense of time lost and events missed makes this a particularly poignant experience.

This reunion period is also an intense emotional experience for children. They will have a strong reaction to the deployment, the reunion, and reintegration, but each child will react differently, even those from the same family. For example, some children may become irritable or cranky, some may be slow to warm up, and others may be clingy or anxious. Keeping your expectations in check will go a long way toward making this transition better for all of you.

Returning from deployment to Ninawa province in Iraq, Cpl. Clinton R. Smith embraces his 3-year-old daughter for the first time in more than six months. *U.S. Marine Corps/Cpl. Corey A. Blodgett*

Many children will have concerns or worries about their own safety, your safety, and being able to rely on you to be there when they need you. Listen for these worries, as they may be expressed in subtle ways, such as in games, pictures, dreams, and indirect comments. For example, children may play out themes of abandonment, war, and death. These moments give you a chance to reassure your children and to talk about things that might be worrying them. Children may also have direct questions for you about the deployment and what happened or could have happened. (Kids are famous for asking "What if?" questions.) Be sure to answer their questions honestly but keep the information appropriate to the child's developmental age and level of understanding. Developmental stages will also be important in predicting what kind of reaction children may have during your reintegration into the family.

Very young children (0–2 years old) may not have a clear idea of who you are, and it will take time for them to get used to you. Knowing this intellectually may not make it any easier when a young child turns away from you or bursts into tears. Try to keep the intensity of the moment in check and keep your expectations low. Your relationship with a very young child can and will be built or rebuilt in time. Children have their own schedules of readjustment, and they will take their cues from those around them.

Children above the age of two years may have an easier time welcoming you home because they appreciate this as an opportunity to celebrate. For them, the initial excitement is very much like a birthday party. When the party is over, they too will need time to adjust. Remember that children need stable and predictable routines in order to feel safe. At first they may have some difficulty dealing with new routines. This is normal. Do not expect young children to immediately accept you as an authority figure. Building acceptance and trust is a gradual process which requires support from other loved ones and caregivers. Again, young children will take their cues from others. It is important for them to see that you are patient, reliable, and trustworthy. They will also be sensitive to any difficulties they might observe between their parents. If children observe parental arguments, they may perceive your return as a cause of conflict and difficulty.

Be prepared for the possibility that your children may at times express rejection. During times of change, children often feel powerless. They sometimes seek to regain a sense of control by choosing not to play with someone. A child might test parental commitment by suggesting they play later instead. You can accept this as a positive opportunity to demonstrate respect and commitment. By remaining present and staying positive and interested—by not getting angry, becoming sad, or walking away—you can pass your child's test of commitment and help your child to overcome insecurity.

When children are older, reunion adjustment problems usually revolve around issues of authority and independence. This is especially true for children who are teenagers. If you have been separated from your child during his or her teen years, it is likely that significant developmental changes have taken place, and parenting strategies must be adjusted accordingly. These changes may feel abrupt at first and can be difficult to accept. Again, it is very important to exercise patience, move forward slowly, and encourage communication. You might have to get humble and take your cues from your spouse or partner.

Some teenagers may seem relatively uninterested in post-deployment reunion. Teenagers are notoriously self-involved. This is normal and developmentally appropriate. Try not to take it personally. In truth, your teenage child is quietly very relieved to see you return safe and sound. He or she might simply experience a sense of awkwardness in expressing emotion.

Children are generally very resilient and adapt well to change when the adults in their lives can provide needed amounts of structure and routine, emotional support, and a safe place to express concerns. Just as you and your spouse take pride in service and sacrifice, your children can be encouraged to take pride in their accomplishments as junior members of a military family. When you return from deployment, they might like to hear you express appreciation and respect for their efforts.

DEPLOYMENT . . . AGAIN

One difficult issue you may face after deployment is the prospect of redeployment. Don't be surprised if preparation for redeployment reignites many or all of the same concerns you felt prior to your first deployment. Questions concerning your motivation, commitment, priorities, and any number of other issues may once again present themselves as difficult, demanding, and all too real. The fact that you already coped with these issues once does not mean they never have to be dealt with again. To the contrary, they may only become more obvious. If so, deal with them at least as carefully as you did before, with special attention to any issues you might wish you had dealt with more effectively prior to your first deployment. Remind yourself that many of your initial concerns were unfounded and remember the ways in which you succeeded in overcoming the many challenges you faced. Trust that you have good reason to be confident in your ability to succeed once again. Finally, remember that although you may be reluctant to rehash old issues, family members and friends also need to build and reinforce their confidence. Again and again, communication is essential.

SPECIAL CONSIDERATIONS FOR RESERVISTS

The unique challenges you face as a reservist do not end when you return home from deployment. The process of reintegrating into your civilian life can be dif-

ficult and often must be undertaken without the social support of fellow reservists who may be geographically separated or overburdened with the demands of
their own lives.

After returning home from deployment, members of a reserve unit might
not meet again at drill for a period of months. Reservists who were deployed
into new units may have little or no opportunity to see or talk with their buddies
again after returning home.

Many reservists are also expected to return to their civilian jobs very soon
after returning home. You might find it necessary to return to work immediately
in an effort to recover from the negative financial impact of your active duty
income or because you cannot afford to take time off from your civilian work.
These and other demands come at a time when you may be struggling in relative
isolation to understand and accommodate your experiences in combat.

The implications of post-deployment isolation and stress can be profound.
You might feel lost, out of place, unappreciated, angry, and disconnected from
the life you once knew as normal and routine at work, at home, and in your
community. It is important for you to know that such feelings and experiences
are quite normal and will usually dissipate gradually over the course of four to
eight months. Meanwhile, it is also important to recognize the potential for
stress-related effects on your overall physical and mental health. You should not
hesitate to seek support from friends, family, and health care providers.

LIFE AFTER THE MILITARY

Eventually, all service members will face the challenge of returning to full civilian life outside of the military. This is yet another transition that demands
readjustment and reintegration. Although military life and service can be challenging, it also provides financial security within a reliable social and professional context. The military takes care of its own in ways that civilian society
does not. Civilian life may seem disorganized, unstable, and unpredictable by
comparison. You may also notice social, political, and economic changes you
could not have imagined possible just a few years earlier. As a result, the transition from full-time military to full-time civilian life may be more complicated
and unsettling than you expect. You can make it easier through advance preparation and planning.

One stark reality of modern civilian life is that few if any civilian jobs offer
long-term security. Civilian workers can no longer expect lifetime security with

An American soldier keeps a watchful eye on a visitor at Contingency Operating Base Basra, Iraq. *National Guard*

a single employer. Retirement plans now emphasize portability. Workers are expected to plan and save for themselves rather than rely upon a single employer or company pension to provide for retirement. When you first face these stark realities, it is normal to feel anxious, lost, and frightened for yourself and your family. Resources such as the Army Retirement Services Office (http://www.armyg1.army.mil/rso/default.asp) are available to smooth your transition.

Military service fosters the development of deep and lasting friendships among service members, family members, and friends. Military units essentially become extended families whose members work together through all aspects of military and family life. Service members in combat forge bonds that extend farther and deeper than those known by civilian coworkers.

When leaving the military, one must deal with leaving behind one's friends and coworkers. Consider this in advance and talk with others about how to stay in touch. Military friendships can and often do last a lifetime. Such friendships can provide essential support through your transition into civilian life, and what you learn through your departure may one day be helpful to others.

At present, the burdens of military service fall upon a fairly small segment of society that comprises our nation's all-volunteer force. As a result, you may find that most civilians do not know much about military life and work. At times, it may appear that most Americans are distracted by issues that seem trivial or selfish in comparison to the hardships and sacrifices you have experienced and witnessed in combat. Your feelings are understandable. It might be helpful to discuss such matters with other veterans who share your experience and understand your perspective. However, it is also important to recognize that while your experiences and perspectives are vital, so too is your connection to a society and people whose liberties you have fought to protect. Communication and respect are necessary to sustain your connection to and good faith among civilian friends, neighbors, and community members. Be conscious of the fact that they can never fully understand what you have seen and experienced. What's more, it may be frustrating or even frightening for them to try. In some cases, it can take years or even decades for society to recognize the implications and full impact of military service and sacrifice.

Civilians might also find it difficult to appreciate your perspective on various political and social issues. Current statistics show that military personnel are more likely to hold politically and religiously conservative views. On a personal level, this disparity may be awkward or uncomfortable. To bridge the gap between military and civilian experience and perspective, it may be necessary for you and others to exercise patience, understanding, and mutual respect. Communication is essential to improved understanding.

In general, civilian Americans now do understand that they should value and respect the service of military personnel and their families. This positive trend stands in stark contrast to the climate that existed after the Vietnam War, when many soldiers were ostracized, insulted, and even accused of criminal behavior by citizens who disagreed with U.S. government intervention in Vietnam. Today American soldiers and their families are accepted by civilians who now better recognize the difference between political policy and military service. It is important that you too be able to draw this distinction. Try to appreciate that while people may express negative sentiment about an unpopular war, they are still able to respect and support your sense of duty, your service, and your sacrifice. New organizations have been established to offer support to service members, veterans, and their families, and there is an increased awareness and attention to problems faced by combat veterans, including long-term effects of traumatic stress and brain injury. Today military veterans can look back on their service with a sense of pride that is reinforced by respect, appreciation, and assistance from fellow citizens.

CONCLUSION

Military personnel who have served, suffered, and sacrificed are understandably motivated to believe that their sacrifices have meaning. Members of the U.S. military serve their country for many good reasons, not the least of which is the desire to do good things in the world. You serve your country because you believe in and wish to defend the essential ideals of freedom and democracy. How, then, should you feel when you hear other people question the value or success of specific military operations? How can you reconcile your sacrifices—and those of close friends—with the suggestion that your mission may have been ineffective or even misguided? What will you feel if the United States loses a war in which you were directly involved?

First, it is important to realize that dissent is not a new phenomenon. In every conflict in which Americans have fought, there has been disagreement with government policy. Even during World War II, some people believed that the United States should not have been involved. During the Vietnam War, political disagreement was intense and sometimes devastating. In a free and democratic society, citizens frequently disagree about government policy and the use of national military resources. Although resistance to government policy may at times be difficult to understand or accept, remember that the right to express and exercise dissent is among the most basic of the freedoms you defend through your military service. Wars are fought on behalf of all Americans using the resources that all Americans work to produce. Citizens have a right and responsibility to carefully consider, evaluate, question, and if necessary challenge policies that expend military resources or put service members' lives at risk. One can question and challenge the decision to send soldiers into combat while also expressing respect and appreciation for the service and sacrifice of soldiers themselves. Most citizens today do recognize that it is not the job of the individual soldier to make foreign policy but rather simply to carry it out.

Remember that you too are a citizen; you are entitled to hold political views and personal beliefs of your own. Ultimately, you will take pride in your military service because you did your job well. You and others should regard your military service not as a political statement but rather as an unconditional demonstration of support for the national defense.

Just as it is important for you to be treated with respect by your fellow citizens, it is also important that you show respect for every citizen's right and responsibility to participate fully in ongoing debate about foreign policy and military operations. Democracy survives by the participation of its citizens. One of the great gifts of American democracy is that it provides for broad, shared control of the military by governmental institutions that are ultimately accountable to the citizenry. Noisy and sometimes messy debate about the use of military force stands in stark contrast to authoritarian military culture.

It is sometimes no easy task to negotiate differences between civilian society and military culture, much less make an effective personal transition between them. It may help you to recognize this challenge as one that may take time and require patience from all concerned.

We have begun the twenty-first century facing great challenges, with our nation's interests defended by a great military. It is up to all Americans—those who have served in the military and those who have not—to preserve and protect our military institutions and celebrate and honor the service and sacrifice of our service members.

APPENDIX
RESOURCES

ARMY

Organization	Description	Contact
Army Human Resources	The official website of the Army Human Resources Policy Directorate. Offers information and resources for soldier health and well-being.	www.armyg1.army.mil /hr/default.asp
Army Behavioral Health	This website offers resources and information regarding mental well-being for soldiers and their families.	www.behavioralhealth .army.mil
Strong Bonds	Information on a unit-based, chaplain-led program that helps soldiers and their families build strong relationships. This service is also for those who are not married.	www.strongbonds.org /skins/strongbonds /display.aspx
Hooah4Health	Army health promotion and wellness website targeted to members of the National Guard and Reserve.	www.hooah4health.com
Battlemind Training	Part of the Walter Reed Army Institute of Research Psychiatry and Neuroscience. It provides links to multimedia resources and information.	www.battlemind.org

Organization	Description	Contact
U.S. Army Family and Morale, Welfare and Recreation	Provides links to many morale, welfare, and recreation community resources for Army service members.	www.armymwr.com
Army Well-Being	Provides links to morale, welfare, and recreation community resources.	www.armyfamilieson line.org
Army OneSource	Provides Army families with articles and information on various topics.	www.myarmylifetoo .com
Army MEDCOM Quality Management Office	Provides information on health issues common to military personnel. Includes a list of resource materials if additional information is wanted.	www.qmo.amedd.army .mil
Army Suicide Prevention Program	Links to resources, news, and information on Army efforts to reduce suicide.	www.armyg1.army.mil /hR/suicide/default.asp
Army Medical Department	Provides an introduction to Army Medical Department organizations. Links to other sites and information on newly implemented changes.	www.armymedicine .army.mil
Army Center for Health Promotion and Preventive Medicine (CHPPM)	Current issues in clinical and preventive medicine, health promotion and wellness, environmental and occupational health, and more.	http://phc.amedd.army .mil/default2.asp
Army Wounded Warrior Program (AW2)	Free 24-hour hotline serves severely wounded, ill, and injured soldiers, veterans, and families, and provides information about benefits, education, and local resources.	www.aw2.army.mil /about/overview.html 1-800-984-8523
Army Well-Being	Serves soldiers, family members, veterans, and retirees with information and resources about health, career, standard of living, community, and personal/family life.	http://www.army well-being.org/skins /WBLO/home.aspx
Family Assistance Hotline		1-800-833-6622

AIR FORCE

ORGANIZATION	DESCRIPTION	CONTACT
Air Force Services Agency	Provides links to morale, welfare, and recreation community resources.	www.afsv.af.mil
Air Force Suicide Prevention Program	Information and tools include Suicide Prevention Program managers, commanders, gatekeepers, etc.	http://afspp.afms.mil/
Life Skills (Mental Health)	A compilation of resources by the Air University Library focusing on issues related to life skills for members of the military.	www.au.af.mil/au/aul /bibs/lifeskills.htm#aaa
Air Force Chaplain Corps	Provides specific resources for chaplaincy care related to deployment for military members and families.	www.usafhc.af.mil
Air Force Family Advocacy Program	Intervention services to address child and spouse maltreatment in military families.	http://www.wpafb .af.mil/library/factsheets /factsheet.asp?id=9390
Air Force Personnel Center (AFPC) Hotline		1-800-616-3775

NAVY

ORGANIZATION	DESCRIPTION	CONTACT
Navy LIFElines Services Network	Focuses on the delivery of quality of life information and services to active and reserve Marines, sailors, and family members.	www.navy.mil/local /lifelines/
Navy Morale, Welfare and Recreation	Provides links to many morale, welfare, and recreation community resources for Navy service members.	www.mwr.navy.mil
Navy Suicide Prevention Program	Tools and resources for leaders and commanders; addresses myths and truths related to sailors and suicide.	www.npc.navy.mil /CommandSupport /SuicidePrevention
Navy and Marine Corps Public Health Center	Information on healthy living, deployment health, and mental health.	http://www-nehc.med .navy.mil/

Organization	Description	Contact
Navy ChaplainCare	Resources for obtaining chaplaincy services, spiritual guidance, and support.	http://chaplaincare.navy.mil/index.htm
Navy Fleet and Family Support Center	Provides information on Navy and community resources for Navy service members, including how to cope with deployment and reunion as well as other personal matters.	https://www.nffsp.org/skins/nffsp/home.aspx
Navy Hotline to Assist IA Families During Deployments		1-877-364-4302

MARINE CORPS

Organization	Description	Contact
Marine Corps Community Services	Provides links to morale, welfare, and recreation community resources.	www.usmc-mccs.org
MCCS Leaders Guide for Managing Marines in Distress	Quick reference designed to help leaders at all levels take care of Marines within the unit who are in distress because of their situation or behavior.	www.usmc-mccs.org/leadersguide
Navy LIFElines Services Network	Focuses on the delivery of quality-of-life information and services to active and reserve Marines, sailors, and family members.	www.navy.mil/local/lifelines/
Navy & Marine Corps Public Health Center	Provides information on healthy living, deployment health, and mental health.	http://www-nehc.med.navy.mil/
"Cover Me" Video	Emphasizes importance of recognizing combat stress; includes messages from the commandant, commander of Joint Forces Command, sergeant major of the Marines Corps, and Marines affected by combat stress.	http://www.semperfifund.org/resources.html

ORGANIZATION	DESCRIPTION	CONTACT
Marine Corps Suicide Prevention Program	Videos and a training curriculum for NCOs, information about suicide in the Marine Corps.	www.usmc-mccs.org /suicideprevent/
Navy ChaplainCare	Resources for obtaining chaplaincy services.	http://chaplaincare.navy .mil/index.htm
Information and Referral Hotline Numbers for Families of Deployed Marines		East Coast Marine Units: 1-800-451-6227 West Coast Marine Units: 1-800-253-1624 Marine Forces Reserve: 1-866-305-9058

GENERAL

ORGANIZATION	DESCRIPTION	CONTACT
Military OneSource	Primary resource for information and many other resource programs for military service members and their families.	www.militaryonesource .com 1-800-342-9647
Real Warriors Campaign	Combats stigma by encouraging service members to increase their awareness of psychological issues.	www.realwarriors.net
National Resource Directory (NRD)	Online tool for wounded, ill, and injured service members, veterans, families, and support personnel. Provides access to more than 11,000 services. Supports recovery, rehabilitation, and community reintegration.	www.nationalresource directory.gov
Defense Centers of Excellence (DCoE) Outreach Center	Answers questions about psychological health and traumatic brain injury for members, families, and veterans of all services, including National Guard and Reserves.	www.dcoe.health.mil /media/DCoE_News /DCoE_Outreach _Center.aspx E-mail: resources @dcoeoutreach.org 1-866-966-1020

Organization	Description	Contact
DCoE Resilience and Prevention Directorate	Promotes "total fitness" for service members, veterans, families, support personnel, and communities.	E-mail: DCoE_Resilience .Prevention@tma.osd.mil
DoD Mental Health Self-Assessment (MHSA) Program	Provides an anonymous self-assessment tool to screen for depression, bipolar disorder, alcohol use, PTSD, and generalized anxiety disorder.	www.militarymental health.org
VA Readjustment Counseling Service Vet Centers	Provides information about services, including individual counseling, group counseling, marital and family counseling, bereavement counseling, alcohol/drug assessments, information and referral to community resources, military sexual-trauma counseling and referral, outreach, and community education.	www.va.gov/rcs
MilitaryHOMEFRONT	The official DoD website for reliable quality-of-life information designed to help troops and their families, leaders, and service providers.	www.militaryhomefront .dod.mil
Seamless Transition	The official Department of Veterans Affairs (VA) website providing information on resources available to returning service members.	www.seamlesstransition .va.gov
Operation Healthy Reunions	Addresses combat stigma among service members, families, and medical staff.	www.nmha.org/reunions
Office of the Assistant Secretary of Defense, Reserve Affairs	Information for Reserve components, including family readiness, income replacement, and TRICARE benefits.	www.defenselink.mil/ra/
American Psychological Association Help Center	Resources and articles on psychological issues that affect physical and emotional well-being.	www.apahelpcenter.org

Organization	Description	Contact
TriWest Healthcare Alliance Behavioral Health Resources	Provides information and resources to recognize and find treatment for many mental and behavioral health issues.	http://www.triwest.com/beneficiary/frames.aspx?page=/unauth/content/ngr/default.asp
National Center for Post Traumatic Stress Disorder	This site is an educational resource on PTSD and traumatic stress for veterans and also for mental health care providers, researchers, and the general public.	www.ncptsd.va.gov/ncmain/index.jsp
National Suicide Prevention Hotline	Free 24-hour hotline available to anyone in suicidal crisis or emotional distress.	1-800-273-TALK (8255)
Deployment Health Clinical Center	Provides information about the health impacts of various deployments and services to improve post-deployment health.	www.pdhealth.mil
DoD Deployment Health and Family Readiness Library	Provides a library of guides, fact sheets, and information for service members and their families on many health and family related issues that face service members.	http://deploymenthealthlibrary.fhp.osd.mil/home.jsp
TRICARE Assistance Program Demonstration	Web-based program expands access to behavioral health services by video chat and instant messaging.	www.tricare.mil/mybenefit/home/overview/special programs/TRICARE assistanceprogram
TRICARE Telemental Health Services	Medically supervised, secure audio-visual conferencing links beneficiaries to offsite providers.	www.tricare.mil/mybenefit/home/Mental HealthAndBehavior/GettingHelp/Telemental Health
Family Advocacy Program (FAP)	Provides links to FAP representatives around the world as well as information about services to troops and family members experiencing domestic abuse and child abuse through prevention efforts, early identification and intervention, support for victims, and treatment for abusers.	www.defenselink.mil/fapmip

ORGANIZATION	DESCRIPTION	CONTACT
Deployed Soldiers Family Foundation	Provides many resources such as information and material items to deployed service members and their families.	http://www.skydive 4free.com/charities /81-deployed-soldiers -family-foundation.php
USA Cares	Military family assistance center provides many services to military personnel and their families.	www.usacares.us
Veterans and Families Coming Home	Provides information and resources focusing on returning veterans, including mental and behavioral health issues.	www.veteransand families.org/home.html
American Academy of Pediatrics "Support for Military Children & Adolescents"	Provides resources such as guides for health care providers and parents.	www.aap.org/sections /uniformedservices /deployment/index.html
American Red Cross	Official website of the American Red Cross. Section for military members and their families includes information for obtaining community-based support, including counseling, financial assistance, and emergency communication services.	http://www.redcross .org/
Substance Abuse & Mental Health Services Administration (SAMHSA)	A Department of Health and Human Services resource with section dedicated to veterans and their families.	www.samhsa.gov
Department of Veterans Affairs Health Care page	Provided by the VA with news and information about care benefits, services, medical centers, various illness, and programs.	http://www.health quality.va.gov/ http://www1.va.gov /health/
Military Veterans PTSD Reference Manual	A reference for veterans suffering from or wanting information on PTSD.	www.ptsdmanual.com
One Freedom	Nonprofit providing services to military personnel and their families. The focus is on returning veterans and their families to help reacclimate to civilian life.	www.onefreedom.org

Organization	Description	Contact
Alliance of Information and Referral Systems (AIRS)	Professional association for Information and Referral providers. It provides resource links and contact information for military personnel and their families.	http://www.airs.org /i4a/pages/index .cfm?pageid=3360
Courage to Care	For military and civilian professionals serving military communities and families; fact sheets on health topics relevant to military life.	www.usuhs.mil/psy /courage.html
The Military Family Network	Works with local organizations for all branches of the military. Special sections are provided for family support, as well as life skills links.	www.emilitary.org
Websites for Heroes	Personalized, secure, password-protected website helps active-duty personnel and families stay connected; features include video and photo galleries, kids' page, message board, calendar, family directory, and news.	www.websitesforheroes .org/
Sesame Street "Talk, Listen, Connect"	Bilingual multimedia initiative to guide families through deployments, homecomings, and other challenges.	http://www.sesame workshop.org /initiatives/emotion /tlc/deployments
After Deployment	Mental wellness resource for service members, veterans, and families; offers assistance to address after-deployment concerns.	www.afterdeployment .org
Warfighter Diaries	Social network platform to foster relationships through short videos and real-life experiences to increase resilience.	www.warfighterdiaries .com/
GI Rights Hotline		1-800-394-9544
Self-Assessment Hotline (Mental Health)		1-877-877-3647

NOTES

Acknowledgments

1. Marjorie Van de Water was a staff writer for the Science Service, a not-for-profit news service founded in 1921 to disseminate scientific and technical information to the public. Today, it is the Society for Science and the Public.
2. Marjorie Van de Water, "Problems faced by a writer in communicating research findings in child development," *Child Development* 19 (1948): 67–75.

Chapter 1: Adjustment to Military Life and Service

1. The Silver Star is the nation's third-highest combat medal. U.S. Army National Guard Sgt. Leigh Ann Hester, a military policewoman in Iraq, was the first American woman to receive the Silver Star for her actions in direct combat, during an enemy ambush on her supply convoy in 2005. Two years later, in 2007, U.S. Army medic Pvt. Monica Brown became the second American woman to receive the Silver Star for heroic actions in combat; Brown risked her life to protect and treat injured comrades while under fire in Afghanistan. A few days after her heroic actions, restrictions on women serving in combat led to Private Brown's removal from the camp where she had been serving with her cavalry unit.
2. Research findings and conclusions concerning effects of gay military service have been reported in peer-reviewed journals such as *Military Psychology, International Security,* and *Armed Forces & Society,* and in reports by researchers at various independent and government agencies including the Defense Personnel Security Research and Education Center (PERSEREC); the

Government Accountability Office (GAO); the Rand Corporation; the National Defense Research Institute; the UK Ministry of Defence; the Palm Center at the University of California, Santa Barbara; the U.S. Military Academy at West Point; and the U.S. Army War College.

Chapter 3: Understanding and Dealing with Stress

1. Surveys from World War II revealed that almost 25 percent of soldiers involved in close combat had urinated or defecated in their pants during a firefight. Most of those who are wounded will lose bowel and bladder control. As disturbing as this may be, it is important to recognize that it is a normal reaction to a life-threatening situation.

INDEX

ABOUT THE AUTHORS

Lt. Col. George R. Mastroianni, USA Reserves (Ret.), served as an experimental psychologist in the U.S. Army and is currently a professor of psychology at the U.S. Air Force Academy. He lives in Colorado Springs.

Barbara Palmer is an experimental psychologist with extensive experience in military research and development and human systems integration. She lives in Dayton, Ohio.

Col. David M. Penetar, USA (Ret.), served as a U.S. Army research psychologist. Currently a psychopharmacologist at McLean Hospital, affiliated with Harvard Medical School, he has remained active in army research and lives in Waltham, Massachusetts.

Victoria Tepe is a behavioral neuroscientist with more than twenty years of professional research experience in academic, medical, and military settings. She lives in Boston.